Mary Page
Peter Guthrie
Sloan Sable

Rules of the Game 2

EDUCATORS PUBLISHING SERVICE

Cambridge and Toronto

Name

Printed in USA

ISBN 978-0-8388-2239-5

14 15 PPG 18 17

CONTENTS

ACKNOWLEDGMENTS

We have long been intrigued with the idea of teaching grammar inductively. Now that we have had the chance to put our ideas on paper, we find that we have not completed the process by ourselves.

To the people behind the scenes who have made this book possible we give our thanks and appreciation:

Jane Knox for her advice and encouragement;
Sarah for her support and good humor;
Doug, Tad, and Scout for time and patience;
Bob, Alan, and Sarah for their encouragement and support; and
Our students for their thoughtful responses to an endless stream of grammar exercises.

INTRODUCTION

In *Rules of the Game* we set out to write a grammar series that would encourage students to discover that grammar is just another name for the patterns that exist in language. In our own teaching, we have discovered that students learn grammar more effectively if they can, in some sense, recreate the process by which rules and definitions have evolved. To achieve this goal, we start each lesson with examples and directed questions, clues to help students see that rules and definitions begin with language and are not handed down from some invisible legislature.

The exercises that follow each lesson rely on both traditional and not-so-traditional approaches. As in most grammar books, we give students sentences and ask them to pick out various points of grammar; but as often as possible we also provide opportunities for students to respond more creatively, using what they have learned. For example, students may be asked to follow sentence patterns, write their own sentences, choose effective modifiers, or combine sentences. Teachers can assign all exercises at the time a concept is introduced, assign the identification problems to diagnose weaknesses, or even save some exercises for those occasions when specific problems occur in student writing.

The lessons are arranged in a way that has worked well with our students. Frequently lessons build on each other: the lesson on the compound sentence appears not long after students have learned what constitutes a sentence and right after they have been introduced to the conjunction. Teachers should feel free, however, to skip around or to supplement in areas where students need more follow-up work. The comprehensive exercises may be used to supplement, to diagnose, or to evaluate.

We hope this series begins a discovery for students that will end only when they can use clear, correct, and effective language to express their ideas.

PART I. REVIEW

1. PARTS OF SPEECH

NOUN: A **noun** is a word that names a person, animal, place, thing, idea, or feeling.

The <u>unicorn</u> gave us <u>companionship</u>.

PRONOUN: A **pronoun** is a word that takes the place of a noun.

<u>He</u> wrote down <u>her</u> assignments. <u>She</u> likes small cars because <u>they</u> use less gas.

VERB: A **verb** is a word that expresses an action or a state of being.

The old man <u>was</u> tired, so his grandson <u>ran</u> ahead.

ADJECTIVE: An **adjective** is a word that describes or limits a noun or pronoun by telling which one, what kind, or how many.*

The guide saw the <u>grassy</u> plain.

ADVERB: An **adverb** is a word that describes or limits a verb, adjective, or other adverb and answers the questions, *How? When? Where?* or *To what extent?***

Jessica read the book <u>very</u> <u>thoroughly</u>.

PREPOSITION: A **preposition** is a word that joins or shows a relationship between a noun or pronoun and some other word in the sentence. It always begins a prepositional phrase.

(<u>Without</u> a doubt), you are the silliest boy (<u>in</u> the class).

INTERJECTION: An **interjection** is a word that expresses a strong or sudden emotion and has no grammatical relationship with other words in the sentence.

<u>Drat</u>! That cat has eaten the fish again.

CONJUNCTION: A **conjunction** is a word that joins words or groups of words of equal rank.

<u>Either</u> you <u>or</u> your brother will make the beds <u>and</u> sweep the floor.

---

*Sometimes nouns and pronouns function, or work, as adjectives in a sentence.
<u>Myra's</u> bag fell off <u>her</u> desk.
**Sometimes nouns function as adverbs.
We took the hamster <u>home</u>.

A. *Directions:* Write the correct part of speech above each of the underlined words in the following sentences. If a noun functions as either an adjective or adverb, label it according to its function.

N for noun	ADV for adverb
PRO for pronoun	PREP for preposition
V for verb	CONJ for conjunction
ADJ for adjective	INT for interjection

                ADV   N

EXAMPLE: Babs walked <u>quickly</u> to the <u>door</u>.

THE REAL JO MARCH: LOUISA MAY ALCOTT

1. Louisa May Alcott <u>was</u> <u>born</u> in <u>Pennsylvania</u> <u>in</u> 1832.
2. <u>She</u> spent most of her <u>early</u> years in Boston <u>and</u> Concord, Massachusetts.
3. May, <u>Elizabeth</u>, and Anna <u>were</u> <u>her</u> three <u>sisters</u>.
4. <u>Louisa's</u> father, Bronson Alcott, is remembered <u>chiefly</u> as a schoolmaster, <u>educational</u> innovator, and transcendentalist philosopher.
5. <u>He</u> counted Henry David Thoreau and Ralph Waldo Emerson <u>among</u> his <u>friends</u>.
6. Bronson's career was <u>not</u> very <u>successful</u>, and the family often did not <u>have</u> enough money.
7. Louisa wrote her <u>first</u> book, *Flower Fables*, <u>at</u> the <u>age</u> of 16.
8. She <u>also</u> worked as a <u>seamstress</u>, governess, <u>domestic</u> servant, and teacher to help her family.
9. During the Civil War Louisa served as an army nurse in a <u>Union</u> hospital, <u>but</u> she <u>soon</u> became ill.
10. *Hospital Sketches* <u>is</u> a book <u>about</u> her <u>experiences</u> as a nurse.
11. The <u>success</u> of this book <u>inspired</u> Louisa to become <u>a</u> <u>writer</u>.
12. She published her first novel, *Moods*, in 1865, and <u>then</u> toured <u>Europe</u> as a "<u>lady's</u> companion."
13. In <u>1867</u> Louisa turned <u>seriously</u> to the field of children's literature for the <u>first</u> time.
14. <u>She</u> became the editor of *Merry's Museum*, a <u>juvenile</u> magazine, <u>that</u> year.

15. <u>Soon</u> *adj.* afterward, she *AV* <u>began</u> to write *Little Women*, her <u>most</u> *adv.* famous book.

16. *Little Women* <u>is</u> *W* a <u>fictionalized</u> *adj.* story <u>about</u> *prep.* Louisa's own childhood and youth.

17. In <u>this</u> *adj.* book she <u>portrays</u> *AV* herself as Jo March and <u>her</u> *pro.* sisters as Amy, Beth, and Meg.

18. *Little Women* was <u>immensely</u> *adv.* popular, <u>so</u> *prep.* Louisa <u>never</u> *adv.* had to worry about money again.

19. She published <u>many</u> more novels <u>during</u> the next twenty years.

20. <u>Alas</u>! Her last few years <u>were</u> <u>filled</u> with sickness and loneliness, <u>and</u> she died on March 4, 1888.

B. *Directions:* Write a sentence for each of the following patterns. You may use articles (*a, an, the*) whenever necessary.

Art/Adj.
The
an
a

N for noun	ADV for adverb
PRO for pronoun	PREP for preposition
V for verb	CONJ for conjunction
ADJ for adjective	INT for interjection

EXAMPLE: ADJ N V PREP N.

The tall boy ran to school.

1. N V N PREP ADJ N.

_____

2. N CONJ N V PREP N PREP N.

_____

3. V PRO V PREP N ADV?

_____

4. ADV ADJ N V PRO ADJ N.

_____

5. INT! PRO V V PREP N.

_____

6. PREP N PRO V ADJ N CONJ ADJ N.

_____

7. N V ADV PREP ADJ N.

_____

8. V   N   V   ADJ   N   ADV?

_____

9. PRO   V   CONJ   V   ADV   PREP   ADJ   N.

_____

10. PREP   ADJ   N   PRO   V   ADV   CONJ   V   PREP   N.

_____

C. *Directions:* Write the correct part of speech above each of the underlined words in the following sentences. If a noun functions as either
an adjective or adverb, label it according to its function.

INT PRO   ADV

EXAMPLE: <u>Help</u>! <u>I</u> can't see <u>well</u>.

THE BEGINNINGS OF CIVIL RIGHTS: 1954–1965

1. The <u>modern</u> civil rights <u>movement</u> <u>really</u> began in 1954.

2. <u>That</u> year <u>the</u> United States Supreme Court <u>decided</u> a case known
   as *Brown v. Board of Education.*

3. In that famous <u>decision</u> the Supreme Court declared that no child
   <u>could</u> <u>be</u> <u>barred</u> from a school as a result <u>of</u> his or her race.

4. <u>In</u> other words, the <u>Supreme</u> <u>Court</u> was saying that <u>America's</u>
   schools should be integrated.

5. In <u>those</u> days blacks in the South <u>had</u> to use separate schools,
   restaurants, and <u>public</u> bathrooms.

6. Black people <u>generally</u> had to sit in the <u>back</u> of buses <u>and</u> to give
   up their seats to whites.

7. <u>This</u> system <u>of</u> separation was called <u>segregation</u>.

8. In <u>1955</u>, in Montgomery, Alabama, a black woman named Rosa
   Parks <u>refused</u> to give <u>up</u> her seat to a white person, and her action
   drew the attention of the entire country.

9. <u>Martin</u> <u>Luther</u> <u>King</u> came to Montgomery and <u>organized</u> a boycott
   of the <u>city's</u> bus company.

10. <u>For</u> months the <u>black</u> people of Montgomery walked, hitched
    rides, and <u>used</u> car pools.

11. <u>Eventually</u> the city gave up <u>and</u> allowed blacks to sit anywhere
    <u>on</u> the buses.

12. In 1957 President Dwight Eisenhower used <u>federal</u> troops to integrate the <u>high</u> <u>school</u> in Little Rock, <u>Arkansas</u>.

13. <u>By</u> the early 1960s <u>many</u> blacks <u>were</u> <u>staging</u> "sit-ins" at restaurants to protest segregation.

14. Many young people, <u>both</u> white <u>and</u> black, traveled to the South to work for the <u>cause</u> of civil rights.

15. <u>Three</u> of <u>these</u> civil rights workers were beaten <u>violently</u> and murdered in Mississippi.

16. A number of other people were killed <u>or</u> hurt in the <u>difficult</u> struggle for <u>freedom</u>.

17. The March on Washington, an <u>enormous</u> rally for civil rights, <u>took</u> <u>place</u> in <u>August</u>, 1963.

18. <u>Thousands</u> of people <u>came</u> to the nation's capital, where Martin Luther King delivered <u>his</u> famous "I Have a Dream" speech.

19. In 1964 the United States Congress <u>finally</u> passed the Civil Rights Act, <u>but</u> the fight for freedom was <u>not</u> over.

20. The <u>next</u> year, in 1965, the Congress went a step <u>further</u> and passed the very important <u>Voting</u> <u>Rights</u> <u>Act</u>.

D. *Directions:* Write ten sentences of your own. Then label the part of speech of every word in each sentence. You do not have to label articles.

EXAMPLE:

1. _____
2. _____
3. _____
4. _____
5. _____
6. _____
7. _____
8. _____
9. _____
10. _____

2. SENTENCES

SENTENCE: A **sentence** is a group of words that contains a subject and verb and expresses a complete thought. In its most basic form this complete thought is called an **independent clause** or **simple sentence**.

World War II began in 1940.

SENTENCE FRAGMENT: A **sentence fragment** is a group of words that does not express a complete thought. Sentence fragments do not finish the ideas or thoughts they begin; they leave you hanging.

Whether you believe it or not.

RUN-ON SENTENCE: A **run-on sentence** consists of two or more sentences that are linked together without the correct punctuation.

I like peanut butter, it is my favorite food.*

COMPOUND SENTENCE: A **compound sentence** consists of two or more simple sentences (independent clauses) joined by a coordinating conjunction.

Plants take in carbon dioxide, and they give off oxygen.

A. *Directions:* In the space at the end of each group of words, write **F** if it is a fragment, **R** if it is a run-on, and **S** if it is a sentence.
EXAMPLE: Oh, on the shelf. __F__

1. When Justine saw the moose. _____

2. Jeff saw Patsy, he waved to her. _____

3. Isadora Duncan was an American dancer. _____

4. Roaring in his ears the wind of the hurricane. _____

5. Big Bill Haywood was a member of the Industrial Workers of the World. _____

6. Although the president didn't understand the reporter. _____

7. Seamus Heaney is a poet, he was born in Ireland. _____

8. Because Nathaniel Hawthorne wrote *The Scarlet Letter*. _____

---

*The correct way to write this sentence is as *two* sentences: I like peanut butter. It is my favorite food.

9. No, you can't have my chocolate. _____

10. Wondering why Norman never called her anymore. _____

11. Katmandu is a city, it is located in Nepal. _____

12. Sergio fixed his dinner, then he ate it. _____

13. Disgusted by the smell of the dead fish. _____

14. Paul Klee was a Swiss artist. _____

15. After Virginia Woolf wrote *To the Lighthouse*. _____

16. On the table sat six mice. _____

17. I bet Yukio a quarter, he won. _____

18. On a raft on the Mississippi many years ago. _____

19. Located in Alabama, the city of Birmingham. _____

20. At the fair I saw Aunt Trudy. _____

B. *Directions:* Revise the following groups of words into one *or* two complete sentences. You may have to add words, capitalize letters, and change or insert punctuation.

EXAMPLE: If I go on Tuesday

If I go on Tuesday, I'll see Albert.

1. Because Helen forgot to bring her money

   _____

2. No, I won't drink the prune juice, I hate it

   _____

3. Skimming down the side of a mountain

   _____

4. Flannery O'Connor was a southern writer, she was born in Georgia

   _____

5. Marlene went to the trial she was a witness for the prosecution

   _____

6. When Candy fell into the vat of chocolate

   _____

7. At the end of the sad song

   _____

8. Emily had terrible table manners, Mrs. Post punished her

   _____

9. If Clyde keeps pestering that cat

_____

10. David felt sick, later he felt better

_____

C. *Directions:* In the space at the end of each group of words, write **F** if it is a fragment, **R** if it is a run-on, and **S** if it is a sentence.
EXAMPLE: Gina saw a moose in Maine. __S__

1. The cat sitting in the window. _____

2. Please bring me some popcorn. _____

3. Elizabeth Blackwell was the first American woman to become a doctor. _____

4. Shielded from the force of the driving wind. _____

5. Rabies is a dangerous disease, raccoons sometimes carry it. _____

6. Did you read the book about Eleanor Roosevelt? _____

7. To reach the top of the mountain and not be able to see through the fog. _____

8. Whales are an endangered species, there aren't many left. _____

9. Did you ever hear Phil Ochs sing, I did? _____

10. When Attila wrecked the house last night. _____

11. One thing was clear, Bilbo had better avoid the dragon. _____

12. I saw some elves slip into the house next door. _____

13. In a hole in the ground there lived a weasel. _____

14. As Holden Caulfield liked to say to anyone who would listen. _____

15. Buy me a candy bar, leave it on my desk. _____

16. Jordan drove like a maniac, Nick just laughed. _____

17. What you don't remember, of course. _____

18. First Joe laughed, then he cried. _____

19. Looking out the window, I spied a baboon. _____

20. Until she can cut the mustard in the kitchen. _____

D. *Directions:* Depending on what type of sentence it is, write **simple** or **compound** in the space after each of the following sentences.
EXAMPLE: I love Lucy. _____**simple**_____

1. Janice and Thor like sailing in the harbor early in the morning.

_____

2. Anabelle decided to be a lawyer but then changed her mind.

   _____

3. Maurice sings, and Hans dances.   _____

4. Hercules had to perform twelve labors.   _____

5. Anthony loves the Scottish Highlands, yet he has not been there
   for years.   _____

6. Johnny Appleseed's real name was John Chapman.

   _____

7. I tried to talk Tina out of it, but she wouldn't listen to me.

   _____

8. On the way to the movies I met Esteban.   _____

9. George Orwell fought in the Spanish Civil War and later wrote a
   book about it.   _____

10. The car broke down, so Dwight had to walk to a gas station.

    _____

11. Mookie and Sean talked and laughed all through the concert.

    _____

12. Peter the Great was a Russian tsar, and Charles I was an English
    king.   _____

13. On Saturday I slept until noon and ate cold pizza for breakfast.

    _____

14. Luigi didn't like his name, but he never changed it.

    _____

15. I ran, and I showered.   _____

16. Gandhi led the movement for Indian independence.

    _____

17. Yesterday Horace swam in the morning, ran in the afternoon,
    and played tennis at night.   _____

18. Many people are allergic to ragweed and have hay fever.

    _____

19. Bill stayed in the treehouse for three years, but no one noticed.

    _____

20. In the reeds at the edge of the river a heron walked and fished
    all morning.   _____

3. PUNCTUATION

END PUNCTUATION: **End punctuation** signals the end of a sentence. Periods, question marks, and exclamation points are the three types of end punctuation. Periods are used at the end of statements (declarative sentences). They are also used at the end of commands (imperative sentences) and indirect questions. Question marks are used at the end of questions (interrogative sentences). Exclamation points are used at the end of exclamations (words or sentences that express strong or sudden feeling).

Where is he going?
He is going to the carnival.
I told him not to go!

COMMA: **Commas**, which are used either alone or in pairs, show you how to read sentences and make them easier to understand. The comma is the most frequently used form of punctuation.*

My older brother brought pizza, popcorn, and soda to the party.

APOSTROPHE: The **apostrophe** indicates the place where letters have been removed in contractions (do not/don't). The apostrophe is also used to form the possessive of nouns (Bill's hat/the girls' team).

Whatever you do, don't sit on Jill's hat.

QUOTATION MARKS: **Quotation marks** indicate the exact words a person is saying. They enclose, or set off, a direct quotation. Quotation marks are also used to enclose the titles of short works such as short stories, short poems, paintings, songs, articles, speeches, chapters, and essays.

Bill shrugged and said, "If you want to go, take the car."

A. *Directions:* Insert the correct punctuation where it is needed in the following sentences. You may add 's when necessary.
EXAMPLE: Why won't you answer, Dave?

1. Carrie drew a fabulous picture Mac said
2. The meal consisted of meat potatoes and salad
3. She wont get out of jail until November 1 1996

---

*For more discussion of the use of the comma, see Book 1.

4. The detective suddenly asked What were you doing the night of the murder
5. Ali said that he couldnt go
6. Run for your life
7. Yes its true I come from Mars Alf admitted
8. Im young Sue said but Im not stupid
9. The old gray donkey stays in his stall all day but he still likes to eat
10. Button up your coat Rudolph
11. On April 12 1998 she flies to Tokyo Japan
12. Yes The Lottery is a frightening story
13. Where are Calcutta Bombay and Madras located Nelson
14. Shirleys mother yelled Stop playing baseball in the living room
15. Who wrote The House at Pooh Corner Raymond the teacher asked
16. Alexander asked why the mice werent in their cages
17. Ivan likes Italian French Chinese and Greek food
18. Darn Ive dropped my glasses in the soup
19. Franco bring that bright red ball here Alice demanded
20. Before she talked with her aunt Tammy didnt know what to say

B. *Directions:* Circle any punctuation marks in the following sentences that are used incorrectly. If a sentence has no errors, write **C** at the end of it.

EXAMPLE: Well, that's a completely different matter.©

1. "I can't hear," Sue said."
2. Jason doesn't know how to use apostrophes.
3. Francine asked "why my car has no wheels."
4. I like lettuce, tomatoes, and, pickles on my sandwiches.
5. The cat stretched it's legs, and jumped off the chair.
6. Help. My hand is stuck in the cookie jar.
7. The state teacher's union called a strike.
8. "I met my husband on, June 9, 1952," Bella said.
9. James's frog has light, green eyes.
10. "Do you have a pen pal in Chile," Patricia asked?
11. "Corey, please put down that fish," Mrs. Stravinsky said."
12. What color were the sheeps' eyes.
13. Benito's address is 6, Oak Street, San Jose, California.
14. Ms. Pippin said "she knew the delivery girl was a spy."
15. Charlie's boss asked him, to type a letter for her.
16. "I would rather have her's than mine," Sammy whined.
17. The small, fluffy kitten attacked the mail carrier.
18. "Don't touch that wire," the electrician shouted.

19. Benjy drove to the mall, and bought a monkey.
20. The women's movement has had an enormous impact on American society.

C. *Directions:* The following sentences are partially punctuated. Insert the missing punctuation marks wherever necessary.
EXAMPLE: "Give that to me," Jill said.

1. Its a long way to Dublin, Ireland.
2. Below the ticket takers were turning people away.
3. Heck Mom said I couldn't stay up all night.
4. "Why does Pedro like marshmallow sandwiches" she asked.
5. Millions of young people read Judy Blumes novels.
6. Did William Faulkner write A Rose for Emily?
7. Theyre the most beautiful paintings in the world.
8. Morty asked me if I'd seen the movie
9. Apart from his uncle Jerrod hadn't told anyone.
10. "Yes I am going to the race," Mopsy replied.
11. "Isn't Antonias black hair beautiful?" Willa asked.
12. The country's chief crops were wheat corn, and oats.
13. Monique entered the contest but she didn't win.
14. "I've read it before," June explained "but I'm reading it again."
15. On January 12, 1979 Rosy won the lottery.
16. "Fiddlesticks" Danny said. "I think that's nonsense."
17. Yes, a flash flood ruined the plumbers convention.
18. Shameem answered "I love to drink tea at Betsy's house."
19. "She's the tall graceful dancer," Boris explained.
20. Melinda's favorite song is entitled Thirsty Boots.

4. SUBJECTS AND VERBS

SUBJECT: The **subject** of a sentence is the noun or pronoun that is doing the action of the verb; it is one of the functions, or jobs, of the noun or pronoun. Subjects and verbs are the building blocks of sentences.

Dustin mowed the grass.

SUBJECT-VERB AGREEMENT: The verb must agree with its subject in number. If the subject is singular, the verb must be singular. If the subject is plural, then the verb must also be plural.

The bear eats fish.
Bears eat fish.

If the compound verb is joined by *or* or *nor*, the verb agrees with the nearest subject:

Neither the teacher nor the students like fire drills.
Neither the students nor the teacher likes fire drills.

Be careful not to confuse the subject of a sentence with the noun or pronoun that follows a preposition:

One of these bats is friendly.
The seats in that theater are uncomfortable.

VERB TENSE: The tense of a verb tells you when the action or state of being took place. The three main tenses are: the present (He plays.); the past (He played.); and the future. (He will play.)

A. *Directions:* Write the subject(s) of each of the following sentences in the space provided at the end.
   EXAMPLE: Harvey carved the pumpkin. _____Harvey_____

THE U.S. GOVERNMENT

1. The Constitution divides the government of the United States into three branches. _____

2. The legislative branch consists of the United States Congress. _____

3. The Senate and the House of Representatives are the two houses of Congress. _____

4. Each state in the country sends two senators to Congress.

   _____

5. On the other hand, the House of Representatives contains 435 members. _____

6. The most important person in the Senate is the Senate majority leader. _____

7. The Speaker of the House leads the House of Representatives.

   _____

8. Senators and representatives debate important issues during Congressional sessions. _____

9. These debates take place in the United States Capitol building.

   _____

10. The president heads the executive branch. _____

11. Presidential elections occur every four years. _____

12. With the help of advisors, presidents choose the members of their cabinets. _____

13. The most important cabinet member is the secretary of state.

   _____

14. Congress has the power to impeach, or to remove, bad presidents.

   _____

15. No president has ever been impeached, but Richard Nixon had to resign in 1974. _____

16. The president and the houses of Congress sometimes disagree about issues. _____

17. The Supreme Court is the highest court in the judicial branch of the U.S. government. _____

18. Nine justices sit on the Supreme Court. _____

19. All of these justices were chosen by presidents. _____

20. The Senate must approve a president's choice of justice, or that justice cannot serve on the Supreme Court. _____

B. *Directions:* Write a sentence for each of the following patterns. Then circle the subject(s) in each of these sentences. You may use articles whenever necessary.

N for noun	ADV for adverb
PRO for pronoun	PREP for preposition
V for verb	CONJ for conjunction
ADJ for adjective	INT for interjection

EXAMPLE: N V N.
Jane ate the pie.

1. N   V   N   ADV.

   _____

2. ADJ   N   V   ADJ   N.

   _____

3. PREP   N   ADJ   N   V   PREP   ADJ   N.

   _____

4. V   PRO   ADV   V   PREP   N?

   _____

5. N   CONJ   ADJ   N   V   N   PREP   N.

   _____

6. CONJ   N   CONJ   N   V   ADV.

   _____

7. INT!   PRO   V   ADJ   N.

   _____

8. V   N   PREP   ADJ   N.

   _____

9. PREP   ADJ   N   N   V   ADJ   N   PREP   N.

   _____

10. ADV   V   PRO   V   ADV   ADJ   N?

   _____

C. *Directions:* Write ten sentences of your own. Then circle the subject(s) in each of these sentences.

EXAMPLE: Spiders like to eat flies.

1. _____

2. _____

3. _____

4. _____

5. _____

6. _____

7. _____

8. _____

9. _____

10. _____

D. *Directions:* Depending on the tense of the verb, write **present**, **past**, or **future** in the space at the end of each sentence.

EXAMPLE: Doreen exercises every day. _____**present**_____

1. Clarence will go to the bar mitzvah on Thursday.

   _____

2. My dad shaves every morning. _____

3.

   _____

4. The governor checked the notes for her speech carefully.

   _____

5. Peter and Sarah live in an old, red-brick schoolhouse.

   _____

6. Next summer Ahmad's family will go to New Zealand.

   _____

7. The Great Potato Famine occurred in Ireland between 1845 and 1849.

   _____

8. One day people will probably live on the moon.

   _____

9. Ms. Driscoll will become head of the law firm this spring.

   _____

10. Vincent Van Gogh painted many pictures of flowers.

    _____

11. Mary now has two children. _____
12. Stan lost his new sneakers last Friday. _____
13. The jury will announce its verdict soon. _____
14. Sao Paulo is the capital of Brazil. _____
15. Dominic loves sardines on toast for breakfast. _____.
16. President John Kennedy served in the navy during World War II. _____
17. Carvings of scarab beetles were popular in ancient Egypt.

    _____

18. When will you be leaving town, Slim? _____
19. Dotty has a collection of 600 rocks. _____
20. The two wild dogs chased Ned up a tree. _____

E. *Directions:* For each of the following sentences, decide which verb in the parentheses agrees with the subject and then circle it.
   EXAMPLE: Bill (is/are) a nice guy.

   1. The enormous frogs (gobbles/gobble) up the cars.

   2. There (is/are) several explanations for Marni's strange behavior.

   3. One of the statues always (falls/fall) over.

   4. Where (has/have) all the flowers gone?

   5. Both Myrtle and Martha (has/have) climbed that mountain.

6. All of those nasty boys (lives/live) near me.

7. Each of the scientists (believes/believe) something different.

8. Sandy and Ted (loves/love) to go to the park on Sundays.

9. There (is/are) a bucket of worms in the basement.

10. Either my mom or my brothers (brings/bring) me home.

11. Everyone here (has/have) seen sheep dance before.

12. Not one of those books (is/are) suitable for children.

13. The news (bores/bore) me.

14. Some of those records (is/are) broken.

15. Neither my friends nor I (am/are) going to Frank's party.

16. Louisa May Alcott's *Little Women* (is/are) my favorite book.

17. Four people in the class (asks/ask) questions.

18. All of those plants (grows/grow) here.

19. Mathematics (is/are) Vernon's worst subject.

20. Neither of the girls (seems/seem) capable of lying.

5. ERRORS

A. *Directions:* Each of the following sentences contains at least one error. Find each error, circle it, and if it needs to be corrected, correct it.
EXAMPLE: I've never been to San Francisco before!

1. Shawn did'nt know his math teachers' name.

2. There are only one kind of candy here.

3. "I bet you can't find me, said Daphne.

4. George Orwell wrote *Homage To Catalonia*.

5. Dolores asked me if I was going to lake Superior for the weekend?

6. Whew. Theyll never find me here.

7. Unlike his aunt Tim love to fly.

8. "Did you take my newspaper," Toby asked.

9. Stanley always wears bright, red clothes.

10. The Statue of liberty is located in new York.

11. Marguerite said "I wont go to the circus."

12. I'll buy a soda, then I'll buy a Hot Dog.

13. One of those cars are worth a fortune.

14. The lawyer's organization contain 106 members.

15. Please give me that cupcake Bailey.

16. Neither the president nor his staff members' likes a scandal.

17. My grandmother, grandfather, and, uncle live in Butte Montana.

18. "Where's the popcorn"? asked the creature from the black lagoon."

19. Tammy and Elmer works in Mr. Smith's store!

20. "He's a wolf in sheeps' clothing" Juanita warned.

B. *Directions:* Each of the following sentences contains at least one error. Rewrite each sentence correctly in the space provided.

EXAMPLE: The two Friends always goes, together.

The two friends always go together.

1. If I travels to italy. Ill buy you some boots.

   _____

2. Which of the chickens have two heads.

   _____

3. "Yes w'ell stop for fast food, Ms. Bosco said."

   _____

4. Either Chet or Ned bring home the bacon, every day.

   _____

5. Emily Brontes "Wuthering Heights" is a terrifying novel.

   _____

6. Do you know if Harry can juggle!

   _____

7. Both Beulah and Petrinka makes wonderful corn bread.

   _____

8. The sleek graceful otter lives on the rivers' edge.

   _____

9. You have'nt got a chance," the other teams capitain said?

   _____

10. The Canadian dancer says that "its cold in Alaska."

    _____

11. Well Im not sure yet, I'll think about it.

    _____

12. "If you have to sing she said, "Sing quietly".

    _____

13. Neither the musicians, nor the director were happy about the instruments'.

    _____

14. Yesterday is my favorite beatles's song.

    _____

15. Because Charles coat has holes. he plan to buy a new one.

    _____

16. "There are no sign of the outlaws now she said.

_____

17. Klaus suddenly screamed be careful.

_____

18. The car lost it's wheels in China Maine.

_____

19. Norman called for toast beets, and Root Beer.

_____

20. "Her's are the best music on the radio," Martins friend announced.

_____

PART II.
NEW MATERIAL

6. DIRECT OBJECT

Read the following sentences and answer the questions in the spaces provided.

A. Sheila threw the chalk at the blackboard.
   1. What word is the subject? _Sheila_
   2. What word is the verb? _threw_
   3. Sheila threw what? _chalk_

B. Bill likes Shirley very much.
   1. What word is the subject? _Bill_
   2. What word is the verb? _likes_
   3. Bill likes whom? _Shirley_

C. Sheila and Bill gave the newspapers to their customers.
   1. What words are the subjects? _Sheila, Bill_
   2. What word is the verb? _gave_
   3. Sheila and Bill gave what? _newspapers_

What do the words *chalk*, *Shirley*, and *newspaper* have in common? If you answered "nothing," look again. *Chalk*, *Shirley*, and *newspaper* all receive the action of their verbs in the above sentences. To put it another way, all three words are affected by the action of their verbs. For instance, in Sentence 1 what did Sheila throw? It isn't too difficult to figure out that the chalk is what Sheila threw. (She certainly didn't throw the blackboard.)

Definition

As you already know, the subject of a sentence is the noun or pronoun that *is doing* the action of the verb. A word that *receives* the action of its verb is called the **direct object**. Since it is one of the functions of a noun, the direct object is always a noun or pronoun. It answers the question *What?* or *Whom?* after an action verb. Although a sentence must contain a subject, not all sentences contain direct objects.

HINTS

A. If you ever have trouble identifying the direct object in a sentence, just ask yourself the question *What?* or *Whom?* For example, in the above sentences, *what* did Sheila and Bill give? *Whom* did Bill like? The answers to these questions—*newspapers* and *Shirley*—are the direct objects in these sentences.

B. Remember, not all sentences have direct objects. If they do, the direct object almost always comes *after* the action verb in the sentence.

For practice, underline the direct objects in the following sentences:

1. Mary printed the banner on the computer.
2. Mr. Metzger returned the tests in class today.
3. Did you receive an A?
4. No, I missed the question on Pearl Harbor.

If you had trouble with sentence 3, a question, turn it into a statement [You received (did receive) an A.] and try again.

DIRECT OBJECT EXERCISES

A. *Directions:* Find the direct object in each of the sentences below and write it in the space to the right.

EXAMPLE: She finally fixed her bike. _____bike_____

THE BRONTES

1. Patrick Bronte lost his wife in 1821. ____wife____
2. He had a parish in Yorkshire, England. ____parish____
3. Reverend Bronte's six children all created fantasy stories during their childhoods. ____stories____
4. Charlotte Bronte published *Jane Eyre* in 1847. ____Jane Eyre____
5. Her sister Anne wrote *Agnes Grey* and *The Tenant of Wildfell Hall.* ____AG and TTWH____
6. Emily Bronte, author of *Wuthering Heights*, loved the Yorkshire moors. ____Yorkshire moors____
7. Branwell Bronte ruined his health with alcohol. ____health____
8. Tuberculosis killed Anne, Emily, and Branwell in the space of a year. ____Anne, Emily, and Branwell____

9. Charlotte visited London several times after the deaths of her sisters and brother. _London_

10. She married the Reverend Arthur Bell Nichols in June, 1854.
Reverend Arthur

B. *Directions:* Write **DO** above the direct object in each sentence below.

DO
EXAMPLE: Jitu loves hamburgers.

WONDROUS BEASTS

1. Medieval lore gives us many accounts of mythical beasts.
2. Cartographers—makers of maps—used their imaginations and covered their maps with all sorts of beasts.
3. Ancient tales relate the habits of unicorns, manticores, dragons, and the fabulous phoenix.
4. Medieval monks and scribes wrote books about imaginary beasts called bestiaries.
5. The illustrations of animals in these books combined scientific information and religious symbolism.
6. In these bestiaries animals served the reader as examples of undesirable behavior.
7. These bestiaries not only told the reader about the habits of mythical beasts, but also gave the reader a moral.
8. Travelers told their audiences different accounts of the unicorn, but all stories gave the unicorn a single horn.
9. This horn contained the unicorn's strength.
10. When in danger, the unicorn threw itself off a cliff and landed without injury on its horn.
11. The manticore's name means "man-eater."
12. Writers assigned the manticore incredible speed and an insatiable appetite.
13. The manticore had the body of a lion, the tail of a serpent, and a triple set of teeth.
14. The phoenix, a bird, represented the sun and only one lived at a time.

15. To reproduce, the phoenix would build a nest, and the sun would set it on fire.

16. The phoenix would throw itself on the fire, and from the ashes would come a new phoenix.

17. In the Middle Ages the dragon represented all evil.

18. Flying at night, dragons sickened people's arms and legs, and later these arms and legs would fall off.

19. The panther's breath, however, could poison a dragon.

20. These tales of fabulous beasts tell us the fears and beliefs of the Middle Ages.

C. *Directions:* Using the words from the columns below, write ten sentences with direct objects. Underline each direct object.

EXAMPLE:	NOUN	VERB
	detective	found
	dog	

The detective found the <u>dog</u> under the shrubs.

NOUNS		VERBS	
cat	teacher	carved	made
book	sales clerk	delivered	disliked
report	Janice	frosted	hid
Mrs. Kelly	woman	sent	rode
hamburger	Henry	drove	mailed
Mr. Olsen	astronaut	gave	wrote
flower pot	dancer	applauded	saw
computer	florist	celebrated	
cake	Tanisha		
jeep	horse		

1. _____

2. _____

3. _____

4. _____

5. _____

6. _____

7. _____

8. _____

9. _____

10. _____

D. *Directions:* Write a sentence for each of the following patterns. Underline the direct object in each sentence. You may use articles wherever you need them.

N—noun	ADV—adverb
PRO—pronoun	CONJ—conjunction
ADJ—adjective	PREP—preposition
V—verb	INT—interjection

EXAMPLE: N ADV V N.
The dog quickly hid the <u>bone</u>.

1. N V N.

_____

2. ADJ N CONJ N V N.

_____

3. PRO V CONJ V N CONJ N.

_____

4. ADJ N CONJ ADJ N V PRO.

_____

5. ADV ADJ N V ADJ N.

_____

6. ADJ N V PRO PREP N.

_____

7. PRO V ADJ N PREP N.

_____

8. V PRO V ADJ N?

_____

9. N V ADJ N ADV.

_____

10. N V PRO PREP ADJ N.

_____

E. *Directions:* Underline the direct objects in the following sentences. Then, in the space provided, rewrite each sentence by replacing the direct object with a new direct object. Add whatever adjectives you need.

EXAMPLE: Myra gave her the <u>balloon</u>.
Myra gave her the furry cat.

1. Marcella survived her fifty-mile hike.

   Marcella survived her fifty-mile swim.

2. James ate his dinner.

   James ate his mom.

3. The class wrote a story.

   The class wrote a play.

4. The canvas covered the canoe.

   The canvas covered the cake.

5. Drop those flowers now!

   Drop those drugs now!

6. Why did you sell your car?

   Why did you sell your books?

7. Mrs. Nguyen drew a horse.

   Mrs. Nguyen drew a person

8. What record did Juana choose?

   What movie did Juana choose?

9. Without help, Mel couldn't change a tire.

   Without help, Mel couldn't change a diaper.

10. Every Tuesday the principal gave us a lecture.

    Every Tuesday the principal gave us a prize.

11. Yikes! Don't bring that thing to class.

    _____

12. Maria put her books on her desk.

    _____

13. Quickly and accurately, Leon squirted catsup on his hotdog.

    _____

14. The well on Jed Clampett's property oozed black oil.

    _____

15. Myra smeared paint over the entire canvas, but John delicately daubed oils only in the corners.

    _____

    _____

16. After school and on Sundays, Natica poured tea for her aunt.

    _____

17. Have you seen my dog?

    _____

18. Aha! Clare spotted the salamander in the garden.

    _____

19. Joseph cracked peanuts with his teeth.

    _____

20. When will the Outing Club show us the film?

    _____

F. *Directions:* Write five sentences of your own that contain direct objects. Label the part of speech of each word in your sentences and underline the direct objects.

EXAMPLE: N   V ADJ N
          Jody loves big <u>fish</u>.

1. _____

   _____

2. _____

   _____

3. _____

   _____

4. _____

   _____

5. _____

   _____

7. INDIRECT OBJECT

Now that you understand and can identify the direct object, you are ready to learn about the indirect object. Each of the following sentences contains an indirect object. See if you can find it by answering the questions in the spaces provided.

A. Leon threw Jeff a party in the basement.

    1. What word is the subject? _Leon_

    2. What word is the verb? _threw_

    3. Leon threw what? _party_

    4. What word is the direct object? _party_

    5. Leon threw a party *for whom*? _Jeff_

B. Katharine gave the car a wash and wax before driving to school.

    1. What word is the subject? _Katharine_

    2. What word is the verb? _gave_

    3. Katharine gave the car what? _wash and wax_

    4. What words are the direct objects? _wash & wax_

    5. Katharine gave the wash and wax *to what*? _Car_

Can you tell what the words *Jeff* and *car* have in common? Look closely. What does each *receive*? Jeff, in a manner of speaking, receives the party, and the car definitely receives the wash and wax. Each word receives the direct object of its sentence.

Definition

Both of the above words—*Jeff* and *car*—are indirect objects. An **indirect object** is a word that *indirectly* receives, or is affected by, the action of a verb. A better way to understand it is to remember that an indirect object receives a direct object. For instance, in the sentences above Jeff receives a party, and the car receives a wash and wax. Like the direct object, the indirect object comes after an action verb and is a function of the noun. It must always be either a noun or pronoun. The **indirect object** answers the questions *To whom? For whom?* or *To what?*

HINTS If you have trouble identifying the indirect object in a sentence, there are two ways you can help yourself:

a. First, you can just ask yourself the questions *To whom? For whom?* or *To what?* the verb does an action. For example, in sentence 2 above, to what did Katharine give a wash and wax? The answer to this question is *car*, the indirect object. Remember, an indirect object can only be a noun or pronoun.

appositives come after Noun/pronoun it re names

b. It is useful to remember two other points about the indirect object. First, the indirect object always comes after the verb and before the direct object. You can see this if you check the sentences above. Second, a sentence cannot have an indirect object unless it has a direct object.

Here is some practice recognizing an indirect object. Underline the direct object in each of the following sentences. Then circle the indirect object in each sentence.

— = IO
O = DO

1. Charlie sent the little red-headed girl a valentine.
2. Helen gave the bookcase a coat of paint.
3. Mr. Fussbinder told me the story of his life.
4. The dirty boy gave himself a bath.
5. The club ordered the girls some new uniforms.

INDIRECT OBJECT EXERCISES

A. *Directions:* Write **DO** above each direct object and **IO** above each indirect object in the sentences below. Not every sentence has an indirect object.

             IO   DO
EXAMPLE: I did not tell him the secret.

1. On Friday he offered us a ride home from the club.
2. Who sent Elise that awful, stale bubblegum?
3. Without a fuss the little boy gave his sister the red dump truck.
4. On my honor I will pay the class treasurer my dues.
5. Quickly tell your classmates the answer to the first question on yesterday's test.
   You = implied
6. Who will buy the team new uniforms?

7. From behind her book Sonya gave her best friend a knowing wink.

8. Mitch sent his valentine card to the girl with the brown hair.

9. During the first really cold weather in December, we cut the Johnsons a Christmas tree.

10. Mrs. Sabich didn't give Isaac permission to sing.

11. Darn! You promised me a bike ride, and now you are giving that other girl a ride!

12. Why didn't you write your grandmother a postcard from Puerto Rico?

13. After a game, Coach Daskalakis always buys his Little League team ice cream cones.

14. Before fishing, my dad gave his new rod to me, and I caught two rainbow trout.

15. At the movies I always buy myself the biggest container of popcorn at the concession stand.

16. In art class the small child made her mother a green macaroni necklace.

17. Every day at 6 A.M. Terry gives his dog Thor a biscuit.

18. Help! I can't buy myself lunch because I forgot my money.

19. Can you lend me some money?

20. Sorry, I don't have enough money for both my lunch and yours.

B. *Directions:* Write five sentences in which you include an indirect object. Label the part of speech of each word in your sentences; then underline the direct object once and the indirect object twice.

     N   V   N ADJ N
EXAMPLE: Roy baked <u>Dale</u> a <u>cake</u>.

1. _____

2. _____

3. _____

4. _____

5. _____

C. *Directions:* Write the indirect object in the space provided at the end of each sentence. If there is no indirect object, write *none* in the space.
EXAMPLE: Sarah gave Kito the book. _____Kito_____

THE GILDED CAGE

1. The French gave Louis XIV the crown at the age of five.
   _____Louis XIV_____

2. Louis gave France the longest reign in recorded history: seventy-five years. _____France_____

3. Under Louis, France became the most powerful country in seventeenth century Europe. _____

4. Powerful nobles caused Louis tremendous difficulty in the early years of his reign. _____Louis_____

5. The nobility gave the king trouble on every issue.
   _____king_____

6. Even the common people of Paris challenged Louis's authority.
   _____

7. Once they gave him a terrible fright by storming through the royal bedroom. _____

8. Eventually Louis offered the nobles new interests to distract them from their plots against him. _____

9. For example, Louis built himself an exquisite and elaborate palace.
   _____

10. The palace of Versailles was the most exciting and important place in all of Europe. _____

11. The palace offered nobles the pleasure of gardens, pools, elaborately decorated rooms, and even a zoo. _____

12. Louis issued them invitations, and they soon forgot about plotting and fighting. _____

13. Louis assigned his visitors elaborate rules of conduct to keep them busy. _____

14. For example, a nobleman would give the door a loud scratch with the little finger of his left hand to announce his presence.
    _____

15. A nobleman would also offer the king a deep bow at dinner.

　　_____

16. Versailles caused nobles new concerns. _____

17. The rule about chairs caused the nobility endless bickering.

　　_____

18. Louis gave the highest-ranking nobility sturdy chairs with arms, while the lowest in rank received three-legged stools.

　　_____

19. Sometimes Louis sent his favorites at Versailles expensive gifts.

　　_____

20. Louis made the nobility a "gilded cage" in the shape of a palace.

　　_____

D. *Directions:* In each of the sentences below, underline the prepositional phrase and change it to an indirect object. Remember, a prepositional phrase begins with a preposition and ends with a noun or pronoun.
EXAMPLE: Maia sent the letter to Mark.
　　Maia sent Mark the letter.

1. Akiko mailed the valentine with the big heart and the arrows to her favorite person.
　　_____Ahiho_____

2. The confused student will ask the question of the teacher.
　　_____

3. The shortstop threw the ball to the second baseman for the beginning of a double play.
　　_____

4. The generous woman bought tickets for the concert for each student.
　　_____

5. At the first game of the season, the former baseball player offered to toss the first ball to the pitcher.
　　_____

6. The friendly old woman offered candy to the trick-or-treaters.
　　_____

7. Kind-hearted Kamala will lend her science notes to the absent student.

_____

8. Her parents granted the privilege of staying out past curfew to Mimi.

_____

9. The wizened old storyteller told the story of the man who came back from the dead to the spellbound children.

_____

10. Before the holiday, Suki sent greeting cards to all of her friends.

_____

E. *Directions:* Write a sentence for each of the following patterns. You may use articles wherever you need them. Underline the direct object once and the indirect object twice in each sentence you write.

N—noun	V—verb
PRO—pronoun	ADV—adverb
S—subject	CONJ—conjunction
PREP—preposition	INT—interjection

EXAMPLE: N V N ADJ N.

Ms. Kim gave <u>Nancy</u> the fountain <u>pen</u>.

1. N V N N.

_____

2. N CONJ V CONJ V N N.

_____

3. ADJ N CONJ V CONJ V N N.

_____

4. ADJ CONJ ADJ N V N N CONJ N.

_____

5. N V N CONJ N CONJ N.

_____

6. ADJ N CONJ ADJ N V ADJ N ADJ N.

_____

7. ADV ADJ N V ADV ADJ N PREP N.

_____

8. LINKING VERB

You have learned about verbs that express action, verbs such as *run*, *sing*, *throw*, or *ask*. Yet not everything you do is an action. Sometimes you don't *do* anything. You just feel, or seem, or *are*. How does a writer tell about a subject who isn't *doing* anything, or express the condition of just *being*? To begin to solve these problems, read the following sentences and answer the questions below.

A. Sol, Benno, and Jill are here.

    1. Does the verb express action or being? _____

    2. What is the subject of the sentence? _____

B. Margaret seems ill.

    1. Does the verb express action or being? _____

    2. What is the subject of the sentence? _____

C. After medical school Kareem will become a doctor.

    1. Does the verb express action or being? _____

    2. What is the subject of the sentence? _____

As you have probably realized, none of the subjects is doing any action, and each verb expresses being. Because there are times when people or things aren't active and don't expend energy, there exists a group of verbs that help to express that condition.

Definition

A **linking verb** is a verb that expresses being and links or connects the subject to either a noun or an adjective. In the examples above, which subject is linked to an adjective? To a noun? If you said *Margaret* is linked to the adjective *ill*, and *Kareem* is linked to the noun *doctor*, you're right. The first sentence does not link the subject to a noun or adjective, but the adverb *here* tells you something about the subject. Even if the subject is linked to an adverb, the verb is still a linking verb.

There are twelve linking verbs. Your teacher may ask you to memorize them so you can easily recognize them in sentences:

be	grow	become	look
seem	smell	appear	taste
stay	sound	remain	feel

The most commonly used of these linking verbs is the verb *to be* (is, am, are, was, were, be).

Some of the above verbs can also be used as action verbs:

The tomato soup tasted bitter.
Jack tasted the strawberry ice cream.

In the first sentence the verb *tasted* links the subject *soup* with the adjective *bitter. Bitter* tells what kind of soup it *is*. In the second sentence, the verb *tasted* tells you what the subject, *Jack,* is *doing.* The noun after the verb (*ice cream*) obviously doesn't identify *Jack;* instead it tells *what Jack tasted* and is a *direct object.* The following linking verbs can also be sued as action verbs:

grow	smell
taste	look
feel	sound

For practice, underline the linking verbs in the following sentences:

1. Mr. Kent has sold most of his land, but he remains a farmer.
2. Working with her friends, Martha is happy.
3. Sula was sick, but she seems stronger now.

LINKING VERB EXERCISES

A. *Directions:* Underline the linking verbs in the following sentences twice.
EXAMPLE: Edgar <u>remained</u> quiet for the entire period.

THE RENAISSANCE

1. In the fourteenth and fifteenth centuries a new way of thinking about people and the world became popular.

2. To us, this period is the Renaissance.

3. Florence, Venice, and Milan were the birthplaces of this new outlook on life.

4. Some people in these cities grew rich from trade and commerce.

5. To the wealthy citizens of these towns, the material objects of everyday life became important.

6. Such non-religious activities as making money and beautifying their cities seemed worthwhile to them.

7. They were also interested in investigating nature and learning about ancient Greece and Rome.

8. Another shift in attitude during the Renaissance was the emphasis on individual ability and people's right to question authority.

9. According to this outlook, it was acceptable to doubt the old solutions to the difficult questions of the past.

10. This new way of thinking appears most clearly in the paintings and sculpture of Renaissance artists.

11. Paintings such as Leonardo Da Vinci's *Mona Lisa* remain exquisite statements of these views.

12. In the *Mona Lisa*, a portrait of a woman, the Renaissance emphasis on the individual is clear.

13. An individual seemed important enough to be the only subject of a painting.

14. The woman in the *Mona Lisa* looks different from all other women and appears thoughtful and slightly mocking.

15. The unusual facial expression is haunting and stays vivid in the memory of the observer.

16. The keen observation of reality and the everyday world became important to artists of the Renaissance.

17. Leonardo's study of geology and air currents was crucial to the *Mona Lisa*'s sense of realism.

18. In addition, the painting appears three-dimensional as a result of Leonardo's use of light and shade.

19. The pieces of fruit in some Renaissance paintings almost smell ripe and taste sweet.

20. The outlook of the Renaissance was much like ours today.

B. *Directions:* Underline each subject once and each verb twice. Then label each verb either AV for action verb or LV for linking verb.

                                        LV   AV

EXAMPLE: In the future, <u>people</u> <u>may become</u> space explorers and <u>travel</u> to other worlds.

1. Elizabeth Blackwell was the first woman doctor in the United States.

2. Stuart felt homesick but remained at camp anyhow.

3. Mrs. Kawasaki did not stay at home.

4. Ernest will become the first seventh grader in the high school marching band.

5. The debating society appeared confident despite the captain's absence.

6. Some families would like to go away for a vacation each summer, yet they often stay at home.

7. Many people use computers in business, and soon, perhaps, the computer will replace the typewriter everywhere.

8. The fried chicken at the picnic tasted delicious, and the cook had many orders for it.

9. Emily grew silent and went home early.

10. With the new speakers the recording of the concerto sounded almost live, and Mark listened to it three times.

11. The smell drifted through the window and filled the cabin.

12. Coming from the swamp, the odor smelled musty.

13. We smelled the odor and left through the back door.

14. Before assuming command of the Union army, U.S. Grant had become the laughing stock of many of his fellow officers.

15. Mrs. Lopez grew roses and chrysanthemums and appeared happy with the results of her efforts.

16. Either you pay your parking tickets or appear in court.

17. At the bakery I tasted a sample, and it tasted delicious.

18. During the Revolutionary War, the Continental Army at Valley Forge was cold, tired, and almost starving, and the fight for independence seemed almost finished.

19. Phillip will look like his father one day.

20. Mr. Henry, as well as his class, heard the tape recording of George's speech, and they thought it sounded clear and coherent.

C. *Directions:* Write a sentence for each of the following patterns. Underline each verb twice and label it LV for linking verb or AV for action verb. You may use articles wherever you need them.

EXAMPLE: S   V   ADJ.

$$\text{LV}$$
Ms. Washington <u><u>is</u></u> late.

1. S   V.

_____

2. S   V   ADJ.

_____

3. ADJ   S   V   ADJ.

_____

4. ADJ   S   V   ADJ   N.

_____

5. ADJ   S   ADV   V   ADJ   N.

_____

6. ADJ   S   ADV   V   ADJ   CONJ   ADJ.

_____

7. ADJ   S   V   N.

_____

D. *Directions:* Write a sentence to illustrate each linking verb. For each linking verb that may be used as an action verb, also write a sentence in which you use it as an action verb. Underline each verb twice and label it LV for linking verb or AV for action verb.

EXAMPLE: smell

$$\text{LV}$$
The small, dirty ragamuffin <u><u>smelled</u></u> musty.

$$\text{AV}$$
He <u><u>smelled</u></u> the freshly-baked muffin.

1. be _____

2. seem _____

3. stay _____

4. grow _____

_____

5. smell _____

_____

6. sound _____

_____

7. become _____

8. appear _____

9. remain _____

10. look _____

_____

11. taste _____

_____

12. feel _____

_____

9. PREDICATE NOUN

In the following sentences underline the verb twice and the subject once. Then answer the questions for each sentence.

A. (After her marriage) my mother <u>remained</u> a teacher.

   1. What word gives another name for the subject?   _teacher_

B. (On Saturdays Sam Wately is the busiest man (in the neighborhood)
                    S   LV

   1. What word gives another name for the subject?   _man_

C. Next year <u>Viola</u> will become a member of the string quartet.
                S LV AV

   1. What word renames the subject?   _member_

D. It is she.

   1. What word renames the subject?   _she_

As you probably noticed, the verbs in the above sentences are linking verbs. After each linking verb comes a word that renames or identifies the subject: *teacher* renames *mother*, *man* renames *Sam Wately*, *member* renames *Viola*, and *she* renames *it*.

Definition

A **predicate noun** (sometimes called a predicate nominative) is a noun or pronoun that comes after a linking verb and renames or identifies the subject. Like the subject, direct object, and indirect object, the predicate noun is one of the functions of a noun. Predicate nouns and predicate adjectives are sometimes called subjective complements because they complement or complete the subject.

A word of caution: Do not confuse the predicate noun with the direct object. (A direct object comes after an action verb) and receives the action of the verb. (A predicate noun comes after a linking verb) and renames the subject:

                             AV   DO
Direct Object: The boy asked a question.

                             LV   PN
Predicate Noun: The boy was the pitcher.

HINT To check whether the noun following a verb is a direct object or a predicate noun, replace the verb with an equals sign (=). If the subject equals, or is the same as, the noun, then that noun is a predicate noun. If the subject does not equal the noun that follows the verb, then that noun *may* be a direct object:

> *Predicate Noun:* The boy was a pitcher.
> boy = pitcher
> *Direct Object:* The boy asked a question.
> boy ≠ question

For practice, underline the subject once and the verb twice in the following sentences. Then label each predicate noun **PN**.

1. Mr. O'Donnell was a city councilor.
2. The once-shy Hazel became a famous actress on stage and in movies.
3. After all these years my grandmother still remains the leader of her hiking club.
4. Someday Isabel will be president of the United States.

PREDICATE NOUN EXERCISES

A. *Directions:* Underline and label the predicate nouns in the following sentences. Underline the verbs twice.

EXAMPLE: Mr. Smith was the president of his club.

1. The brick and stone building was the oldest library in the city.
2. Even after injuries Jessie and Chris remained goalies.
3. Mr. Garcia and Ms. Josephs both were coaches for the team.
4. On Monday Terry became the first violinist in the state to win the competition.
5. In his new job Daniel will be a carpenter.
6. Most of the cars were convertibles, but some were sedans or station wagons.
7. The advertisement in the paper was an original one.
8. The painting was an oil painting from the eighteenth century.
9. The woman in the black pants seems to be the one in charge.
10. Which cookies are the ones baked by your mother?
11. Often whoever appears to be the leader isn't really in charge.

12. Willa was to have been the guest speaker, but she became ill.

13. Will the lead in the play be you or I?

14. *Death of a Salesman* and *All My Sons* are plays written by Arthur Miller, a great American playwright.

15. The children became campers at the annual jamboree.

B. *Directions:* Write two sentences for each of the following patterns. Use an action verb in the first sentence and a linking verb in the second. In each sentence label the verb as either an action verb (AV) or a linking verb (LV). Label direct objects (DO) and predicate nouns (PN). Use articles wherever you need them.

EXAMPLE: S V N.

          AV   DO

    Misty hit the ball.

          LV   PN

    Leonard was the teacher.

1. ADJ S V ADV.

_____

2. ADJ S CONJ S V ADV.

_____

3. ADJ S V N.

_____

4. ADJ S V ADJ N.

_____

5. ADJ CONJ ADJ S V ADJ N.

_____

C. *Directions:* Write ten sentences of your own that contain predicate nouns. Then label the linking verbs (LV) and the predicate nouns (PN).

                  LV   PN

EXAMPLE: Corinne is a successful engineer.

1. _____
2. _____
3. _____

4. _____
5. _____
6. _____
7. _____
8. _____
9. _____
10. _____

10. PREDICATE ADJECTIVE

Underline the subject once and the verb twice in the following sentences. Then answer the questions that follow.

A. (At the party) Ms. Hu appeared happy. *[PA]*
   1. Is the verb an action verb or a linking verb? _Linking_
   2. What word describes the subject? _happy_

B. My gym locker smells musty. *[PA]*
   1. Is the verb an action or a linking verb? _Linking_
   2. What word describes the subject? _musty_

C. (After the test) Earl felt good. *[PA]*
   1. Is the verb an action or a linking verb? _Linking_
   2. What word describes the subject? _good_

As you have probably discovered, the above verbs are all linking verbs. None shows action, but each describes a *state* of being. After each linking verb in the above sentences comes a word that describes the subject: *happy* describes *Ms. Hu*, *musty* describes *locker*, and *good* describes *Earl*. What is the part of speech of each word that appears after the linking verb? You've probably guessed correctly that *happy*, *musty*, and *good* are all adjectives.

Most verbs help to make a statement about the subject. Since a linking verb tells a state or condition, the linking verb is ideally suited for creating a description of the subject. As you have already seen, each of the adjectives that follows a linking verb in the above examples describes the subject.

Definition

A **predicate adjective** is an adjective that comes after a linking verb and describes or *limits* the subject. As mentioned before, predicate nouns and predicate adjectives are sometimes called subjective complements because they complement or complete the subject.

A word of caution: do not confuse a predicate adjective with an adjective that describes a predicate noun.

Anne Frank was courageous.
He was a courageous patient. *[PN]*

Both sentences contain linking verbs. In the first sentence the adjective after the linking verb describes the subject, *Anne Frank*; therefore, it is a predicate adjective. In the second sentence the adjective describes the word *patient*; therefore, it modifies *patient*, not the subject, and is not a predicate adjective.

HINTS

A. If the adjective after a linking verb appears in front of a noun, it usually modifies that noun and is not a predicate adjective.

ADJ   N

He is a courageous patient. (What kind of patient?)

B. Replacing the linking verb with an equals sign (=) can help you discover whether a sentence contains a predicate adjective and what it is:

> My mother looks pretty.
> My mother = pretty
> predicate adjective = pretty

In the above sentence *pretty* is the predicate adjective. But now look at a different kind of sentence:

> My mother is here.
> My mother ≠ here

There is no predicate adjective in this sentence because *mother* is not the same as *here*. The word *here* is, in fact, an adverb.

For practice, underline the subject once and the verb twice in the following sentences. Then label each predicate adjective.

1. The food in the cafeteria tasted bitter.
2. Despite a heavy workload, Marina remains calm and happy.
3. My sneakers stayed dirty even after a thorough washing.
4. That woman seems angry.
5. Matt's new book is terrific.

PREDICATE ADJECTIVE EXERCISES

A. *Directions:* Place a predicate adjective in the blanks below.

EXAMPLE: The man in the washing machine became wishy-washy .

1. The man who rode on the train all night seemed tired .

2. The salad with the rotten tomatoes tasted _gross_____.

3. The skunk smelled _stinky_____.

4. The racing car driver whose car was in front remained
_calm_____.

5. When she sees the *A* on her test, Mary will become
_excited_____.

6. Roses are _purple_____; violets are _magenta_____.

7. The sick child's mother appears _exhausted_____.

8. The water in the heater stays _hot_____ for twelve hours.

9. Ernestine felt _~~an~~ in pain_____ after she had had her braces
put on.

10. With the bad phone connection, Steve's voice sounded
_raspy_____.

11. After spending twelve consecutive hours dancing, Judy and Henry
looked _sweaty_____.

12. When she heard the news about her dog's disappearance, Ms.
Hanley grew _overjoyed_____.

B. *Directions:* Write a sentence for each of the following patterns. Underline the predicate adjective in each sentence. You may use articles wherever you need them.

EXAMPLE: N V ADJ.
The girl seems <u>happy</u>.

1. N V ADJ.

_____

2. N V ADV ADJ.

_____

3. ADJ N V ADJ CONJ ADJ.

_____

4. ADJ N ADV V ADJ.

_____

5. ADJ N V ADV ADJ.

_____

6. N V ADV ADJ CONJ ADJ.

_____

7. ADV   ADJ   N   V   ADJ   CONJ   ADJ.

_____

8. ADV   ADJ   N   PREP   N   V   ADV   ADJ   CONJ   ADJ.

_____

C. *Directions:* In the sentences below write **S** over each subject and **PA** over each predicate adjective.

EXAMPLE: Miss Roberts was ill.
(S over Miss Roberts, PA over ill)

1. (After chopping wood,) Alexandra is always tired. *(PA over tired)*
2. (With three consecutive victories,) the field hockey team appeared confident (on the field.) *(PA over confident)*
3. (Entering the dark and gloomy Gothic mansion,) Ms. Witherley felt fearful and uneasy. *(PA over fearful, PA over uneasy)*
4. (With the addition (of choco-bits,) these brownies taste much more delicious. *(PA over delicious)*
5. The band made up (of four tubas,) twelve piccolos, and one glockenspiel sounded peculiar, and the audience did not remain in the auditorium for long. *(PA over peculiar)*
6. (As she grows older,) Katherine will grow more responsible and independent. *(PA over responsible, PA over independent)*
7. Mr. Daniels took the sweaters (out of summer storage;) they smelled musty. *(PA over musty)*
8. My mother saw the scattered flowers and remained calm. *(PA over calm)*
9. (When the vase broke) she become furious. *(PA over furious)*
10. I am nervous only when I go (to the dentist.)

D. *Directions:* Underline the predicate nouns and predicate adjectives in the following sentences. Then label them **PN** or **PA**.

EXAMPLE: Alex is a clever girl.
(PN over girl)

HOMESTEADER'S HOUSE

1. Pioneer homesteaders were very important (in the settlement of the Great Plains.) *(PA over important)*

2. The promise of free land became a magnet for thousands of home-steaders.

3. By 1900, plowing and sowing five acres of land was the basic requirement for acquiring free land.

4. Today visible traces of the early homestead days are almost non-existent.

5. The Brown family's house in the Badlands of South Dakota is an eighty-year-old prairie homestead.

6. This homestead is a small, dark house made from bricks of hard sod or dirt.

7. Sod home construction was popular on the plains.

8. The buffalo grass seemed practical for dry roofs because of its densely tangled roots.

9. The three-room sod house was quite small for a family of three.

10. The construction of the living room seems quite different from the other rooms.

11. Apparently the living room was an old mining shack.

12. On the Brown homestead water did not become available for many years.

13. Carrying water was a long, hard job.

14. Grazing was also difficult in this barren land.

15. Poverty remained a constant problem.

16. Many of these homesteaders or "sodbusters" did not remain satisfied with this way of life.

17. Prairie dogs remain the sole inhabitants of the land.

18. Today the Browns' old homestead looks cozy and quaint with its quilts and crocheted doilies.

19. The abundant prairie sage smells sweet.

20. Life was desperately hard for the Browns, and the colorful bed quilt and crocheted doilies are misleading evidence.

11. APPOSITIVE

To discover what an appositive is, read the sentences below and answer the questions that follow them.

A. I looked for my cat Groucho.

    1. What is the name of the cat? _____

    2. What part of speech is the cat's name? _____

B. I left my book, *The Flame Trees of Thika*, in my locker.

    1. What is the name of the book? _____

    2. What part of speech is the book title? _____

C. What present did the team give to Mrs. Chauncey, their favorite referee?

    1. What is another name for Mrs. Chauncey? _____

    2. What part of speech is this other name? _____

What do all of the above words have in common? Of course, since they are nouns, they must name. But the above nouns have a special naming function. Each of these nouns gives *another* name to a noun already stated in the sentence: Groucho renames cat, the *Flame Trees of Thika* renames book, and referee renames Mrs. Chauncey. In addition, each of the nouns you listed above provides more information about the noun it renames. Notice, too, where these renaming words appear. Each comes either right after, or almost right after, the word it renames.

Definition

An **appositive** is a noun or pronoun that comes directly after another noun or pronoun and renames that noun or pronoun. Appositives add information about a particular noun or pronoun. Since an appositive is yet another one of the functions of a noun, it is always a noun or pronoun.

A word of caution: do not confuse the appositive with the predicate noun. The predicate noun always comes after a linking verb and can rename only the subject. The appositive can appear in a sentence with either an action or linking verb, and it can rename not just the subject but any noun or pronoun:

                  S   LV   PN

Predicate Noun: Mr. Lowell remained a gardener.

                  S   AV   IO   APP   DO

Appositive: Mrs. Ojeda gave Mr. Lowell, the gardener, his shovel.

                  S   APP   LV   PN

Both: Mrs. Ojeda, his employer, was a woman of taste.

ESSENTIAL AND NONESSENTIAL APPOSITIVES

An appositive may be set off by commas, as in the following sentence:

I left my book, *The Flame Trees of Thika*, in my locker.

The title of the book, *The Flame Trees of Thika*, gives you extra information, but it is not necessary to the sentence. The fact that the person left the book in the locker is what this sentence is about. The book's name is set off by commas to let you know it is not essential to the meaning of the sentence. You could leave out the appositive and the sentence would still make sense. Now look at these two sentences:

1. Myra's dog, Daisy, is her only pet.
2. Ray has three cats. Ray likes his cat Groucho best.

As you probably noticed, the appositive *Daisy* is set off by commas. Like *The Flame Trees of Thika*, this word gives you extra information—in this case, the name of Myra's dog. Since this appositive is not essential, you could leave it out and the sentence would still make sense. You may also have noticed that the appositive *Groucho*, in sentence 2, is not set off by commas. Can you guess why? If you think about it for a minute, you'll see that the word *Groucho* is *essential* to the meaning of sentence 2. If it weren't included, you wouldn't know which of his cats Ray likes best. In fact, the sentence doesn't make any sense without this word.

Remember, an appositive *that is not essential* to the meaning of a sentence is set off by commas. An appositive *that is essential* to the meaning of a sentence is not set off by commas.

HINT If you have trouble telling the difference between a predicate noun and an appositive, keep this fact in mind. A linking verb separates a predicate noun from the noun it renames; however, there is *never* a verb between an appositive and the noun it renames.

For practice, underline the appositives in the following sentences:

1. The teacher, Mr. Posrat, ran the class by bribing his students, all seventh graders, with jellybeans.

2. On her day off, Monday, Lois Lane will go with her friend Jimmy Olson to meet Superman, her hero, and to fight the arch enemy Lex Luthor.

APPOSITIVE EXERCISES

A. *Directions:* Underline the appositives in the following sentences.

EXAMPLE: Nai-Hui insisted upon taking me to see the movie *The Attack of the Killer Bees*.

FUNKY JAZZ

1. In the early 1900s America witnessed the birth of an original style of music, jazz.
2. The music of Black America—blues, spirituals, and ragtime—had the most influence on its development.
3. Blues songs were the most popular style of Black American folk music and often described a sad state of mind, "the blues feeling."
4. Spirituals, religious folksongs, were sung by both blacks and whites at church revival meetings.
5. Ragtime was composed for the piano and emphasized a "ragged" style of music, syncopation.
6. "The Entertainer," a ragtime song by Scott Joplin, used choppier rhythms than ordinary music.
7. After 1900 two black musicians from New Orleans, King Oliver and Jelly Roll Morton, fused these different musical traditions to form a new type of music, jazz.
8. Unlike most music, jazz emphasized a style of creating music by ear, improvisation.
9. As in other art forms, such as dance and drama, improvisation in music means that it is created spontaneously or on the spur of the moment.
10. One of the most famous jazz musicians of our time, Louis Armstrong, began his career by playing on street corners and in cafes in New Orleans.
11. Armstrong popularized a type of jazz singing, the scat song, in which he invented melodies spontaneously by imitating the sounds of instruments.
12. Jazz itself eventually included many different styles of music—boogie-woogie, swing, and bop.
13. The popular music of today, rock and soul, is rooted in the traditions of jazz.
14. "Funky" and "cool," jazz terms, reflect the influence of jazz on language today.

15. The widely different styles of three composers—Maurice Ravel, Igor Stravinsky, and George Gershwin—reflect the enormous influence of jazz on classical music in the twentieth century.

B. *Directions:* Write a pair of sentences for each noun listed below. In the first sentence of the pair, *modify* the listed word with an adjective, and in the second sentence rename the word with an appositive. Label each adjective **ADJ** and each appositive **APP**.

EXAMPLE: farmer

      ADJ
1. The tan farmer worked all day in the fields.

         APP
2. The farmer, Pat O'Connell, tilled the fields from morning to night during planting season.

book	author	country
cartoon	team	friend
actress	singer	
animal	stereo	

1. _____

_____

2. _____

_____

3. _____

_____

4. _____

_____

5. _____

_____

6. _____

_____

7. _____

_____

8. _____

_____

9. _____

_____

10. _____

_____

C. *Directions:* Use an appositive to combine each of the pairs of sentences listed below.

EXAMPLE: That man is funny. That man is Dan Smith.
That man, Dan Smith, is funny.

1. The lawyer was Ms. Ross. She pleaded the case with great eloquence.

   _____

2. Jumbo was an elephant. He was the main attraction in P. T. Barnum's circus.

   _____

3. Last night my brother saw that new movie. The title was *The Zombies Eat Out But Don't Enjoy Sushi.*

   _____

4. James Agee's only novel was *A Death in the Family.* It won the Pulitzer Prize.

   _____

5. London is located on the Thames River. It is the capital of England.

   _____

6. Mr. Tanaka drove his new car downtown. His new car was a sedan.

   _____

7. The meteorologist tracked the hurricane up the coast. Its name was Luther.

   _____

8. Juana phoned the florist for flowers. She ordered roses and chrysanthemums.

   _____

9. Marla took her driver's test on Tuesday. It was her birthday.

   _____

10. Miss Phelan sent Kenneth a box of baseball cards. He is her nephew.

    _____

D. *Directions:* Underline the appositives in the following sentences. Then place commas where they are needed.

EXAMPLE: Luka's cousin, Jean, is her only relative.

1. My uncle Bob took me to the hockey game.
2. The fisherman's boat Lucky Lady chugged to its home port with a hold full of fish.
3. Mrs. Sweeney the police officer shopped only at the Tasty Treats Super Market.
4. I asked my friend Sheila for the notes for the class I missed.
5. Hera's husband Zeus had a roving eye and was constantly seducing mortal women.
6. One young maiden Europa turned herself into a bull in order to avoid Zeus's advances.
7. Hera a vindictive goddess often spied on her husband and on the other gods and goddesses.
8. The colors of the football team the Pittsburgh Steelers are also my favorite colors gold and black.
9. Henry gave the gavel to John the club president.
10. Heather sent her father his favorite candy yogurt-covered peanuts.

12. OBJECT OF THE PREPOSITION

In the sentences below, place parentheses around each **prepositional phrase** (see below for definition) and then answer the questions that follow.

A. (Throughout her life) Marie Curie searched (for scientific truths)

    1. What kind of word appears at the end of each prepositional phrase?

       ~~fruits~~ = nouns

B. (With her husband) she discovered the radioactivity (of thorium)

    1. What kind of word appears at the end of each prepositional phrase?

       nouns

C. She was awarded two Nobel prizes, one (for her work) (in physics) and one (for her work) (in chemistry)

    1. What kind of word appears at the end of each prepositional phrase?

       nouns

What do the listed words have in common? Yes, each comes at the end of a prepositional phrase. Also, the words *life, truths, husband, thorium, work, physics,* and *chemistry* are all nouns. Every prepositional phrase in the above sentences ends in a noun.

Definition

As you know, a prepositional phrase is a group of words that begins with a preposition and ends with a noun or pronoun. Because a preposition joins a noun or pronoun to the rest of the sentence, every prepositional phrase must contain a noun or pronoun. The noun or pronoun that appears at the end of a prepositional phrase is called the **object of the preposition**.

You have already learned that nouns may function as subjects, direct objects, indirect objects, predicate nouns, and appositives. Now you know that nouns have still another function—as objects of the preposition.

HINT Always place parentheses around the prepositional phrase in a sentence before you try to determine which nouns are objects of the preposition. This method will keep you from getting confused by nouns with other functions.

For practice put parentheses around each prepositional phrase in the sentences below; then underline each object of the preposition.

1. (Throughout seventh grade) Angela swam every day (at the school pool.)
2. (For many years) Dennis lived (on Chestnut Street), but then his family moved (across town).
3. The china (on the back shelf) was washed (before every holiday meal.)
4. The player (with the red and blue uniform and cap) slid (into third).

OBJECT OF THE PREPOSITION EXERCISES

A. *Directions:* Place parentheses around each prepositional phrase in the following sentences. Then underline the objects of the prepositions.
   EXAMPLE: The leader (of the group) left the room (for ten minutes.)

DEADLY TRIANGLE

1. (In a section) (of the Atlantic Ocean) (near Florida) known as the Bermuda Triangle, some mysterious events have occurred.
2. (According to one report) more than a hundred planes and ships have vanished (into thin air.)
3. (Since 1945) hundreds (of lives) have been lost (in this area.)
4. Many planes were (in radio contact) (at the moment) (of their disappearance.)
5. Other reports cited a number (of strange developments) before the planes vanished.
6. Pilots have complained (during these transmissions) (about wild fluctuations) (in their compasses and gyroscopes.)
7. (In other instances) severe storms have been reported (during excellent weather conditions.)
8. Strangely enough, many (of these incidents) have occurred (around Christmas time.)
9. The most celebrated case involving the dangers (of the Bermuda Triangle) concerns the disappearance (of five Avenger torpedo bombers) (in 1945.)
10. (According to reports) a group (of navy planes) took off (from Fort Lauderdale) (in excellent weather conditions) (for a two-hour patrol) (over the Atlantic.)
11. Near the time of their return, the navy base began receiving strange messages from these planes.

12. Apparently the pilots were lost and could not recover their sense of direction.
13. The flight leader reported to the base during this emergency that even the ocean didn't look right.
14. Within a short time communication with these planes was broken forever.
15. No remains of the planes or pilots were ever found in the ocean or on nearby beaches.
16. A rescue plane with a crew of thirteen also disappeared without a trace.
17. Scientists have offered numerous explanations for these occurrences, including theories about space warps, sea quakes, and alien scouting parties from other planets.
18. The most recent research, however, has presented logical, ordinary explanations for each incident.
19. In the case of the navy planes, the mistaken judgment of the flight leader seems to have been the most important cause of the disaster.
20. In most media accounts of incidents occurring in the Bermuda Triangle, reports about these navy planes were sensationalized and falsified.

B. *Directions:* Put parentheses around each prepositional phrase. Then write **OP** above the object of the preposition in each phrase.

EXAMPLE: (Without his sister,) James could not complete the

assignment (for English class.)

CHILD OF COURAGE

1. (In 1934) Otto Frank moved his wife and two daughters (from Frankfort) (to Amsterdam.)
2. (By this time) Hitler had already begun to attack people who opposed his policies.
3. Soon afterwards Hitler put (into effect) his anti-Jewish program; Jews were dismissed (from public office) and the civil service.)
4. At first many Jews lost all means (of livelihood) then Jews were segregated (from Aryans.)

5. Because of this oppression, Otto Frank, from an old and distinguished Jewish family, left Germany and began a new business in Holland.

6. During the next few years Otto's family lived a normal life without fear of Nazi persecution.

7. In 1940 the German invasion of Holland brought Hitler's anti-Jewish program to Holland and into the world of the Franks.

8. Under German occupation, Jews were prohibited from any form of transportation except walking, and they could shop only between the hours of three and five in certain stores.

9. Jews also had to be indoors by eight o'clock at night and were forbidden to visit places of entertainment or to participate in public sports.

10. Jews could only attend all-Jewish schools, so Anne and Margot Frank, Otto's daughters, went to the Jewish Lyceum.

11. The roundup of Amsterdam's Jews for shipment to concentration camps began in February, 1941.

12. By the time Margot was called up in July, 1942, Otto, with some Dutch friends, had already prepared a hiding place for his family within his warehouse.

13. For two years the Franks and four other Jews lived in silence above the daily bustle of the warehouse.

14. Throughout the time within the "secret annex," Anne poured her thoughts and feelings into her diary.

15. She wrote both about the daily happenings in the "secret annex" and beneath her window and about the war around Amsterdam and throughout Europe.

16. Anne kept the diary until the discovery of the hiding place and her murder by the Gestapo, Hitler's secret police.

17. The Gestapo scattered the diary around the annex, and Dutch friends found it and kept it until after the war.

18. These friends gave it to Otto Frank, the only survivor from the annex, upon his return from the concentration camp at Auschwitz, and it was first published in 1947.

19. The diary has been translated into many languages besides English, and two plays have been written from it.

20. Through the diary, today's reader discovers the courage of a young girl living under almost impossible circumstances.

C. *Directions:* Write a sentence for each of the prepositions listed below. Place parentheses around each prepositional phrase. Label the object of the preposition in each phrase.

EXAMPLE: underneath   OP

           Mrs. Gomez placed the can (underneath the faucet.)

1. with _____
2. like _____
3. in _____
4. over _____
5. between _____
6. down _____
7. except _____
8. to _____
9. during _____
10. upon _____
11. off _____
12. until _____
13. of _____
14. under _____
15. at _____

D. *Directions:* Write a sentence following each of the sentence patterns listed below. Put parentheses around each prepositional phrase. Label each object of the preposition. You may use articles wherever you need them.

EXAMPLE: (PREP   N)   N   V   (PREP   N.)

                     OP   OP

       (During the winter) the boy ran (around the track).

1. N V (PREP N.)

_____

2. N (PREP N) V ADV.

_____

3. ADJ N V (PREP N.)

_____

4. ADJ N (PREP ADJ N) V (PREP ADJ N.)

_____

5. N (PREP N CONJ N) V.

_____

6. N V (PREP N) CONJ (PREP N.)

_____

7. N (PREP N) V (PREP N) CONJ N.

_____

8. ADJ N (PREP ADJ N) V (PREP ADJ N CONJ N.)

_____

9. (PREP N) ADJ N V.

_____

10. (PREP N) V ADJ N.

_____

13. FUNCTIONS OF THE PREPOSITIONAL PHRASE

Read the sentences below and answer the questions that follow them:

A. Michael danced with grace.

    1. Rewrite the sentence, replacing the prepositional phrase with an adverb, but keeping the original meaning.

    _____

B. Kamala walked home.

    1. Rewrite the sentence, replacing the adverb with a prepositional phrase, but keeping the original meaning.

    _____

C. The dog with the floppy ears chased the cat.

    1. Rewrite the sentence, replacing the prepositional phrase with an adjective, but keeping the original meaning.

    _____

D. The loud-voiced manager yelled constantly.

    1. Rewrite the sentence, replacing the adjective with a prepositional phrase, but keeping the original meaning.

    _____

> **Definition**
> A **prepositional phrase** always functions as either an adjective or an adverb. When it acts as an adjective, it modifies a noun or pronoun—like an adjective. When it acts as an adverb, it modifies a verb, an adjective, or another adverb—like an adverb. Most adverbial prepositional phrases modify verbs.

The prepositional phrase differs from the adjective and the adverb only in that the entire phrase, from the preposition to the object of the preposition, is the modifier. The adjective and the adverb are usually single or hyphenated words. Notice the difference in the sentences below:

ADV
Michael danced gracefully.

ADV
Michael danced (with grace.)

ADJ
The floppy-eared dog chased the cat.

ADJ
The dog (with floppy ears) chased the cat.

A word of caution: always place parentheses around the entire prepositional phrase before you determine whether it is functioning as an adjective or an adverb. The parentheses will serve as a reminder that the entire phrase is the modifier.

HINTS

A. The adjective phrase almost always appears right after the noun it modifies, while the adverb phrase can appear either before or after the word it modifies:

ADJ
The teacher (with the eyeglasses) walked quickly to class.

ADV
The teacher walked (with great haste) to class.

ADV
(With great haste) the teacher walked to class.

B. Introductory prepositional phrases, those at the beginning of sentences, are nearly always adverb phrases:

ADV
(After school) my friends and I will go to the game.

ADV
(Around the rock) the rugged rascal ran.

For practice put parentheses around each prepositional phrase in the following sentences and label it either ADJ (for adjective) or ADV (for adverb). Then draw an arrow to the word it modifies.

1. For twenty years Odysseus travelled throughout the Mediterranean.
2. Odysseus met a monster with one eye, creatures with the tops of women and the bottoms of birds, and his dead mother.
3. The man at the tollbooth paid his fare.

FUNCTIONS OF THE PREPOSITIONAL PHRASE EXERCISES

A. *Directions:* Put parentheses around the prepositional phrases in the following sentences. Then label them **ADJ** or **ADV** depending on their function.

           ADV   ADV
EXAMPLE: He hit the ball (against the wall), and it bounced (over the fence.)

PIONEER IN GENE RESEARCH

1. In 1983, at the age of 81, Barbara McClintock was awarded the Nobel Prize for Medicine.
2. This choice surprised no one in the scientific community.
3. Today nobody can conduct research in genetics without an understanding of her work.
4. For a long time, however, scientists scorned her research.
5. Barbara McClintock first published her ideas about genes and chromosomes in 1951.
6. For decades she worked in isolation with her corn plants.
7. Dr. McClintock's theory differed from the popular view of genes as immovable beads on a string.
8. As a young student, Barbara had little interest in anything except science classes.
9. To Barbara the most worthwhile time was spent in reading and thinking.

10. After high school Barbara became an interviewer in an employment agency.

11. Her mother did not want her to go to college and become a college professor.

12. She also complained about Barbara's "unfeminine" behavior.

13. With grim determination Barbara tried to educate herself and spent all of her free time at the library.

14. Finally her parents relented and sent her to Cornell University in Ithaca, New York.

15. From the first day of classes, Barbara was thrilled by her courses in biology.

16. Eventually Barbara obtained her Ph.D. from Cornell.

17. She then conducted research in genetics at the Cold Spring Harbor Laboratory in Washington.

18. At Cold Spring Harbor, Barbara was usually ignored by her colleagues.

19. Barbara McClintock is only the third woman ever to be awarded an individual Nobel Prize in the sciences.

20. The other women were Marie Curie, in 1911, for her work with radium, and Dorothy Hodgkins, in 1964, for her work in chemistry.

B. *Directions:* Put parentheses around each prepositional phrase. Label it either ADV for adverb or ADJ for adjective.

                                ADJ   ADV

EXAMPLE: The chicken (with the brown feathers) flew (around the house).

1. At lunchtime, Ms. Walters calmly opened her yellow plastic lunchbox with the purple armadilloes on it.

2. Within it she found a once-scrumptious cream cheese and olive sandwich underneath a rather large Macintosh apple.

3. She held the moist, flattened square in her hands, and tears spilled from her eyes and over her eyelashes.

4. "Oh no!" she said. "What am I to do without my daily sustenance? Why was the apple on top?"

5. Noisily bemoaning her fate, Ms. Walters, with streaming tears, stumbled toward the principal's office.

6. The principal, a young man of extreme sensitivity, sat at his desk and spread papers over his desktop.

7. He looked up at the door and saw the disturbed Ms. Walters stumble into his office and perch near the fish tank.

8. "May I help you with something?" asked the principal. "Do you wish to feed the fish or perhaps speak to me?"

9. "I want to know why chalk smells like roses, why students do everything but read and, most of all, why the apple was on my sandwich. Can you help me?" sobbed the teacher.

10. The principal, now confused beyond all measure, didn't know how to console the teacher and to help her with her philosophical questions.

11. Moving his chair near the window, he gazed for inspiration at the football field shimmering in the afternoon brightness.

12. Slowly, just behind his eyes and below his hairline, an idea began to form.

13. In the dim recesses of his brain, an idea took hold.

14. Something chocolate, something white was the answer to the harassed teacher's dilemma, and slowly he stood up and walked around his desk.

15. At the file cabinet he reached beneath the handle, pushed the lock, and opened the drawer marked, "H—O."

16. From the rear, between Oregon and Oriole, he pulled a package.

17. He had carried this package throughout his career, but now the time had come to pass it on to another.

18. He carried the package toward the wild-eyed woman, now crouching behind the desk, and gently said, "Would one of these help?"

19. Ms. Walters peered into the young man's warm brown eyes and saw his compassion.

20. With a smile on her lips, she reached for the package and put an Oreo between her lips. Gone was all memory of the sandwich.

C. *Directions:* Put parentheses around each prepositional phrase. Label it either ADV for adverb or ADJ for adjective.

ADV   ADJ

EXAMPLE: (At the movies) I saw a woman (with green hair).

1. Like her brother, Eliza became captain of the swim team.
2. Many of the books read by the class were about the American West.
3. Behind Mrs. Mallard trailed the ducklings.
4. Across the river stood the house with the wide porch and green shutters.
5. Besides the usual American fare, the buffet offered many foods from other countries.
6. The small table near the stairs had on it an old vase of considerable value.
7. On the shelf and near the table were many small glass animals.
8. Above the shelf hung the picture with the gilt frame.
9. The distant figure among the trees stood still briefly and then walked toward the shore.
10. Without a doubt John is the best candidate for class president, but many may vote against him.
11. With whom will you travel during summer vacation?
12. Beyond today no one knows what will happen.
13. The boat floundered amid the huge waves and almost ran into a rock.
14. The librarian at the desk said I could keep the book until Tuesday.
15. Toward dawn the train came through the tunnel and crept down the mountain.
16. According to the evening weather report, the wind tomorrow will be blowing off the ocean.
17. Will you put the letter into the envelope and place it on top of the desk?

18. Some of us got to class on time.

19. It appeared at the time that the problem could not be solved by only one person.

20. In spite of her friends' warning, Elaine went to the beach.

D. *Directions:* Write one sentence for each of the prepositional phrases listed below. Put parentheses around each phrase and label it either ADV for adverb or ADJ for adjective.

EXAMPLE: on the roof   ADV

       Hank saw a pigeon (on the roof).

1. behind the steely grey eyes

_____

2. among the lions

_____

3. beneath the trapdoor

_____

4. except for the cat

_____

5. without his friends

_____

6. with blood-red fingernails

_____

7. in the maroon racecar

_____

8. like a cave

_____

9. on the speeding train

_____

10. on the cloud

_____

14. SEMICOLON

By adding only one mark of punctuation, make the meaning clear in the sentences below:

1. The rain began to pour during the game the spectators were soaked.
2. Dick tripped accidentally he broke the vase.
3. The baby toddled with glee she smeared jelly on the wallpaper.

Without the correct punctuation the meaning of each of the above sentences is unclear. When did the rain begin? Did Dick break the vase accidentally or on purpose. Was the baby a gleeful toddler or a gleeful finger painter? Correct punctuation would help answer each question.

Each of the sentences above is a run-on. To correct each one you could add a period and a capital letter to make two distinct sentences. You could also add a coordinating conjunction and a comma; however, since the instructions say to make just one addition, the only possible addition is the semicolon:

1. The rain began to pour; during the game the spectators were soaked.
   The rain began to pour during the game; the spectators were soaked.
2. Dick tripped; accidentally he broke the vase.
   Dick tripped accidentally; he broke the vase.
3. The baby toddled; with glee she smeared jelly on the wallpaper.
   The baby toddled with glee; she smeared jelly on the wallpaper.

Definition

A **semicolon** is a punctuation mark used in place of a coordinating conjunction to join two independent clauses and to emphasize the close relationship between the two.

With coordinating conjunction: Harriet wrote detective novels, and her husband, Peter, was a detective.
With semicolon: Harriet wrote detective novels; her husband, Peter, was a detective.

Remember, only use a semicolon to join two independent clauses that have a close relationship:

Correct: My father plays the flute; my mother plays the piano.
Incorrect: The leaves will change color; my dog Fido wanted to be fed.

Unless the color of the leaves affects Fido's appetite, these two independent clauses have nothing to do with each other and should not be joined by a semicolon. They should be two separate sentences separated by a period.

The semicolon is also used before such words as *accordingly*, *besides*, *consequently*, *hence*, *however*, *moreover*, *nevertheless*, *otherwise*, *therefore*, *then*, and *thus*. Because these words emphasize a close relationship between two independent clauses, the semicolon is the logical punctuation to use:

> I was late for class; however, the class hadn't begun the test yet.
> The snow has begun; consequently, the roads will be slippery.

Note that each connecting word is not only always preceded by a semicolon, but is also always followed by a comma.

Finally, unlike commas and periods, semicolons are *always* placed *outside* closing quotations marks:

> The man said, "Put down your pencils"; however, I did not listen.
> Ann used words like "bizarre" and "horrifying"; Biff was frightened.

For practice, place semicolons where they are needed:

1. I did not study for the test consequently, I may not do very well.
2. Herbert entered the car carefully he put on his seat belt.
3. Todd didn't appreciate the political cartoon moreover, he disagreed with the editorial.
4. Annabel placed the golf ball on the green she took her first shot.

SEMICOLON EXERCISES

A. *Directions:* Insert semicolons in the sentences below in the correct places.
EXAMPLE: Most of the students were ill; however, the class still met.

CHINA

1. China has the largest population of any country in the world about a fifth of all the world's people live there.
2. It is also the world's third largest country only Russia and Canada are larger.
3. China has a wide range of climates for example, there are subarctic, tropical, and desert regions within its borders.
4. China's official name is the People's Republic of China it is sometimes referred to as the Chinese People's Republic.
5. The People's Republic was declared in 1949 after years of war and foreign invasion therefore, the task of constructing a modern industrial state has been monumental.

6. Those years of chaos were caused by the final disintegration of the Chinese empire imperial China had provided the Chinese with order and prosperity for the preceding 2,000 years.

7. China has the world's oldest living civilization accordingly, its written history dates back 3,500 years.

8. The Chinese were the first to develop such items as the compass, gunpowder, and paper consequently, they take tremendous pride in their past.

9. The accomplishments of the imperial period are remarkable for instance, they developed an efficient government, built great cities, and created stunning works of art and literature.

10. Occasionally nomadic invaders conquered China however, these invasions had little effect on Chinese civilization.

11. In the nineteenth century the Chinese empire started to decline that is, China experienced misgovernment, peasant unrest, and domination by foreign powers.

12. Finally, in 1911 discontent produced a revolution a republican form of government was established.

13. The republican government attempted to establish order and prosperity nevertheless, it failed to improve peasant conditions.

14. The most important task for the Republic was to provide peasants with land instead, it supported powerful landlords and wealthy businessmen.

15. In these conditions Chinese communism gained popularity with factory workers moreover, they soon took up the cause of the peasant as well.

16. After 1949 the new communist government succeeded in gaining popular support it reduced the gap between rich and poor and improved the standard of living.

17. In the late 1960s and early 1970s the communist government promoted an upheaval known as the Cultural Revolution furthermore, this revolution was accompanied by economic disaster.

18. Today a different communist government continues to struggle with the problems of overpopulation and modernization much work remains to be done.

19. China is seeking technical help with these problems from outside the country hence, contacts between China and the United States have increased dramatically.

20. The result is an exciting exchange consequently, the Chinese benefit from American technology, and Americans become better acquainted with one of the oldest and richest civilizations ever to exist.

B. *Directions* Write ten sentences of your own that include semicolons.
EXAMPLE: I caught a bat; it bit me.

1. _____
2. _____
3. _____
4. _____
5. _____
6. _____
7. _____
8. _____
9. _____
10. _____

15. COLON

The following letter contains many mistakes. Underline the errors.

> Dear Mr. Briggs,
> I read about your pharmacy in *Pharmacy Can Be Fun* 3, 11. I was most impressed and would like to apply for a part-time job. I can start work after school every day at 3;15 and work until closing at 9-00. I have had experience doing the following. babysitting, mowing lawns, and running errands. My former employers were pleased with my work, and they would be glad to write me recommendations.
>
> > Sincerely,
> > Jerry Tinsdale

As you may have discovered, the writer of the above letter has forgotten to use needed colons. If he had, he would have written:

> Dear Mr. Briggs:
> I read about your pharmacy in *Pharmacy Can Be Fun* 3:11. I was most impressed and would like to apply for a part-time job. I can start after school every day at 3:15 and work until closing at 9:00. I have had experience doing the following: babysitting, mowing lawns, and running errands. My former employers were pleased with my work, and they would be glad to write me recommendations.
>
> > Sincerely,
> > Jerry Tinsdale

Let's hope that the job Jerry has applied for requires little writing or that Mr. Briggs is a forgiving employer.

Definition

A **colon** is a punctuation mark used to indicate that something is following. To put it another way, it is a signal that says, "Note what follows."

The rules for using a colon are few and, except for the last one, fairly straightforward:

1. A colon should appear after the salutation in a business letter:

> Dear Mr. Briggs:
> Dear Sir or Madame:

2. A colon should appear between volume and number, or between volume and page number, of a periodical:

> *Atlantic Monthly* 97:6
> *Newsworthy* 3:12

3. A colon should appear between the hour and the minutes when you write the time:

> 3:15 p.m.
> 12:00 midnight

4. A colon should appear before a list of specifics, especially after expressions like *as follows* and *the following*:

> Please read the following:
> *Lord of the Flies*
> *A Separate Peace*
> *Tex*
> *I Am the Cheese*

You have probably been following the third rule since you could tell time. The first two rules are equally straightforward. An easy way to remember the fourth rule is to remember that a colon is used every time you want to signal the reader to take special note of something.

Like semicolons, colons are *always* placed *outside* closing quotation marks:

> Doris said the following cities are "must see": London, Paris, and Rome.

For practice, add colons where needed in the following sentences:

1. I arrived at Kennedy International Airport at 6 30.
2. The article on John Keats can be found in *Poets International* 5 7.
3. Please do the following chores walk the dog, pick up your room, and set the table.
4. The passage read at the service today was Exodus 2 1-10.

COLON EXERCISES

A. *Directions:* Insert colons in the correct places in the following sentences.

EXAMPLE: Esther ate the following for dinner: potato chips, ice cream, and cheese doodles.

FACTS ABOUT WORLD WAR II

1. World War II began with the German attack on Poland on September 1, 1939, at 4 45 A.M.

2. In this same year, 1939, the following appeared for the first time nylon stockings, baseball on television, and Steinbeck's *The Grapes of Wrath*.

3. The most popular songs that year were the following "God Bless America," "Over the Rainbow," and "I'll Never Smile Again."

4. Discouraged by England's refusal to surrender, Hitler later opened a second front by invading the Soviet Union on June 22, 1941, at 3 00 A.M.

5. Later that year the Japanese extended the fighting to the Pacific Ocean by launching a surprise attack at 7 55 on a Sunday morning against the American naval base at Pearl Harbor.

6. Nineteen forty-three was a turning point for the Allies (England, France, and the United States), who forced the Germans to retreat from the following places Africa, Sicily, and Italy.

7. The final defeat of Hitler began with the launching of the largest amphibious operation in military history on June 6, 1945, at 6 30 A.M. against the German army occupying France.

8. On this same day, June 6, in other years, the following occurred the assassination of Robert Kennedy (1968), the first American naval victory over Japan (1942), and formation of the Chrysler Corporation (1925).

9. On May 7, 1945, known as VE Day, the German military surrendered and agreed to stop fighting in Europe at 11 01 P.M. on May 9.

10. Later, Japan surrendered, shortly after the first atomic bomb was dropped by the United States on Hiroshima on August 6, 1945 at 8 15 in the morning.

11. The following teams won the World Series during American involvement in the war New York Yankees, St. Louis Browns, St. Louis Cardinals, and Detroit Tigers.

12. During World War II the most popular movies were the following *Casablanca*, *The Wizard of Oz*, and *Bambi*.

13. An article on Dwight D. Eisenhower, Commander in Chief of the Allied forces, can be found in the *New York Review of Books*, 33 30.

14. *Time* magazine, 128 48, published an article discussing Stalin, leader of the Soviet Union during World War II.

15. You can even find an article in the *Smithsonian* magazine, 16 25, on how the war in France changed football forever.

B. *Directions:* In the following letter correct the errors in the use of the colon and semi-colon.

   EXAMPLE: Dear Sir;

   Dear Sir:

126 Hooker Avenue
White Plains, New York
June 9; 1987

Scurry Furry Food Company
404 Oakwood Street
Cleveland; Ohio

Dear Sir or Madame,

    I am inquiring about your advertisement in *Hamster's Quarterly* 12;1. You stated that you sell hamster food; but do you sell the following; Hamster Heavenly Pellets, Domestic Rodent Tidbits; and Lettuce Alone? Also do you have any advice about the best time to feed a hamster? I have been feeding mine in the morning at 4.30; I find that my hamster: Hepzibah, often suffers from indigestion; she has trouble digesting her Yummy Tummy Tidbits. I have pondered this matter for some time: I cannot solve it by myself and now need your help.

                Sincerely;
                James T. Cork

C. *Directions:* Rewrite the following sentences to correct any errors in punctuation.

    EXAMPLE: Nandy lives in England: George does too.
                Nandy lives in England; George does too.

1. The train always arrives punctually at 4:30 p.m.; and I make sure I am there to see it.

    _____

2. The reading: that the student chose, was Exodus 2-12.

    _____

3. When coming to camp, please bring the following, three pairs of shorts, three shirts, and one pair of rubber-soled shoes, all should be labelled with your name.

    _____

    _____

4. The school bus has a flat tire: therefore, we must go to the game in cars.

    _____

5. The young athlete practiced everyday, moreover, she studied strategy.

   _____

6. The letter began, "Dear Mrs. Johannson:" and ended, "Yours truly;".

   _____

7. Moira did not study as long as she wanted : consequently, she did not do as well as she would have liked.

   _____

8. Please do the errands as follows; drop the cake off at Mrs. Bellows's house, take the clothes to the cleaners, and then buy the groceries.

   _____

   _____

9. The minister began the sermon by reading from John 2;23.

   _____

10. Mr. Jefferson yelled enthusiastically the team played hard.

    _____

PART III.
COMPREHENSIVE
EXERCISES

16. FUNCTIONS OF THE NOUN

A. *Directions:* Write the function of the underlined noun or pronoun in the space provided at the end of each sentence. For example, if the underlined word is a predicate adjective, write *predicate adjective* in the space.

EXAMPLE: He chose a dog. _____direct object_____

1. I gave my <u>mother</u> a small elephant. ___indirect obj.___
2. Dolly sent a long letter to <u>Mitzie</u>. ___Obj. of prep.___
3. The <u>pitcher</u> threw the ball hard. ___S___
4. Santa Claus is a fat, jolly <u>man</u>. ___PN___
5. My friend <u>Antoine</u> is a sailor. ___app.___
6. The yellow <u>bill</u> of the owl stands out in the dark. ___S___
7. The ancient car is <u>rusty</u>. ___PA___
8. Sally told <u>me</u> an exciting story. ___io___
9. In the <u>clearing</u> sat a fierce bear. ___Obj. of prep.___
10. Betsy, a young <u>girl</u>, hates parties. ___app.___
11. Morris drank two <u>glasses</u> of lemonade for dinner. ___dO___
12. Clarence is an extremely skillful <u>dancer</u>. ___PN___
13. After a day at work, Mom seems <u>tired</u>. ___PA___
14. We threw <u>them</u> into the lake. ___dO___
15. After the movie <u>you</u> looked sad. ___S___
16. John Buchan wrote <u>*The Thirty-Nine Steps*</u>. ___do___
17. He seems an old <u>man</u> now. ___~~io~~ PN___
18. Germaine threw a pail of water at her <u>brother</u>. ___Obj. of prep___
19. <u>Millions</u> of bison died in the 1870s. ___S___
20. Ella read <u>her</u> a book about ants. ___~~pro~~ io___

B. *Directions:* Label the function of each underlined noun or pronoun in the following sentences. Label predicate adjectives, too.

S for subject   PN for predicate noun
DO for direct object   PA for predicate adjective
IO for indirect object APP for appositive
OP for object of the preposition

EXAMPLE: <u>Jill</u> winked slyly at <u>Ted</u>.
    S   OP

io before do

1. My brother, <u>Pablo</u>, is a successful <u>artist</u>. [APP, PN]
2. Hank gave <u>Dana</u> a record for her <u>birthday</u>. [IO, OP]
3. <u>One</u> of these cats ate my <u>canary</u>. [S, DO]
4. May <u>we</u> go to the <u>store</u> now? [S, OP]
5. The food on my <u>dish</u> looks <u>disgusting</u>. [OP, PA]
6. Tasha is a <u>vegetarian</u>, so she does not eat <u>pork</u>. [PN, DO]
7. <u>Hundreds</u> of people slept late on Monday, the <u>holiday</u>. [S, APP]
8. The buckets of <u>sand</u> immediately put out the <u>flames</u>. [OP, DO OP]
9. Brett remembered <u>her</u>, but <u>she</u> had forgotten him. [DO, S]
10. The fierce fox gave the <u>horse</u> a <u>bite</u> on its <u>leg</u>. [DO or IO, PN do, do]
11. The news sent <u>Cal</u> into a <u>rage</u>. [IO, OP]
12. My sister <u>Anisha</u> is <u>beautiful</u>. [APP, PA]
13. There is the <u>man</u> with the <u>beard</u>. [S PN, OP]
14. Haley made <u>Kathryn</u> a spinach <u>sandwich</u> for lunch. [IO, DO]
15. This <u>sentence</u> is certainly a simple <u>one</u>. [S, PN]
16. In the dark <u>everything</u> appears <u>larger</u>. [S, OP]
17. The old dog is mangy, but <u>we</u> love <u>him</u> anyway. [S DO, IO DO]
18. Tara's cousin <u>Clyde</u> is a stamp <u>collector</u>. [APP, PA]
19. The end of the <u>holiday</u> saddened <u>Juan</u>. [OP, DO]
20. Howie went to the <u>concert</u>, but it was <u>terrible</u>. [OP, PA]

C. *Directions:* Underline the nouns and pronouns in the following sentences. (<u>Don't</u> underline possessive pronouns.) Then label the function of each of these nouns and pronouns. Also, underline and label any predicate adjectives.

S for subject
DO for direct object
IO for indirect object
OP for object of the preposition

PN for predicate noun
PA for predicate adjective
APP for appositive

EXAMPLE: John sent his sister a letter.

THE SIOUX AND THE BUFFALO

1. The Sioux are a group of Native Americans.
2. Originally they were located in Minnesota.
3. In the seventeenth century other peoples pushed the Sioux into the Great Plains.
4. Millions of buffalo roamed the plains in those days.
5. The buffalo played an important role in the lives of the Sioux.
6. The Sioux, a nomadic people, built their way of life around the buffalo.
7. Buffalo herds gave them food, tools, clothing, and shelter.
8. The buffalo shaped their ceremonies, mythology, and art, too.
9. The Sioux followed the buffalo herds around the plains.
10. They could not take many possessions with them.
11. They hunted the buffalo in groups.
12. Sometimes they surrounded the animals.
13. They also stampeded the buffalo over cliffs.
14. A man's success in Sioux society depended on his hunting ability.
15. Even young boys played hunting games.
16. Sioux women gathered wild plants, dried the meat, and treated the buffalo hides.
17. The Sioux, a skillful people, made clothes, blankets, and tepees from the hides.
18. Buffalo bones gave them tools, utensils, and ceremonial ornaments.
19. Never before or since has one animal provided a people with so much material and inspiration.
20. Sadly, the destruction of the buffalo in the late nineteenth century also destroyed the Sioux's culture and way of life.

D. *Directions:* Each of the following problems indicates a particular function of the noun or pronoun. (One indicates the predicate adjective.) Make up sentences of your own that contain the indicated functions. Then underline the word that functions in that manner.

EXAMPLE: subject

      <u>Ann</u> flew to Miami.

1. indirect object

   _____

2. object of the preposition

   _____

3. predicate noun

   _____

4. appositive

   _____

5. direct object

   _____

6. predicate adjective

   _____

7. object of the preposition

   _____

8. predicate noun

   _____

9. subject

   _____

10. appositive

    _____

17. PARTS OF SPEECH

A. *Directions:* Write the correct part of speech above each of the under-lined words in the following sentences. If a noun functions as either an adjective or adverb, label it according to its function.

N for noun   ADV for adverb
PRO for pronoun   PREP for preposition
V for verb   CONJ for conjunction
ADJ for adjective   INT for interjection

                    V PRO   CONJ
EXAMPLE: Tom, pass me the bread and butter.

FOR THE UNIONS: MOTHER JONES

1. Mary Harris Jones was born in Cork, Ireland, in 1830.
2. Her father emigrated to the United States in 1835.
3. He sent for his wife and children soon after that.
4. Young Mary attended school in Toronto, Canada.
5. Mr. Harris was a railroad worker there.
6. When she was older, Mary taught in a convent school in Michigan.
7. Then she moved to Chicago and started a dressmaking business.
8. In 1861 Mary Harris married a man named Jones.
9. He belonged to a labor union.
10. Six years later her husband and four children died in an epidemic of yellow fever.
11. Grief-stricken, Mary worked as a nurse, but then resumed her dressmaking career in Chicago.
12. After she lost all her possessions in the Chicago Fire of 1871, Mary began to devote her time to labor unions.
13. In her opinion these unions could help working people.
14. In those days many workers had to work long hours in dangerous conditions.
15. From 1880 on, Mary committed herself to the labor movement.
16. She led strikes and held educational meetings for poor workers.
17. Mary was especially concerned about the plight of coal miners.

89

Parts of speech:

noun
pronoun
verb
adverb
adjective
interjection
preposition
conjunction

Noun Functions:

subject
DO
IO
PN
APP
OP
(PA)

adj. q's:
what kind?
which one?
How many?
(whose?)

adv. q's:
How?
when?
where?
why?
To what extent/
under what conditions?

18. The owners of coal companies in West Virginia threatened her life on many occasions.

19. She also raised the public's awareness of the evils of child labor.

20. Known around the country as "Mother Jones," Mary lived to the age of 100.

B. *Directions:* Label the part of speech of every word in the following sentences. If a noun functions as either an adjective or adverb, label it according to its function. You do not have to label articles.

N for noun	ADV for adverb
PRO for pronoun	PREP for preposition
V for verb	CONJ for conjunction
ADJ for adjective	INT for interjection

EXAMPLE: I gave a sled to my mother.

1. Smallpox is a highly contagious disease.
2. How do you feel about slime molds?
3. My goodness! I did not see that enormous tree.
4. Julian and Nadia are going to the old museum.
5. Have you ever read about Davy Crockett?
6. We took grandma to the football game on Sunday.
7. Julia read us an extremely frightening story.
8. Ouch! That crocodile bit me on the foot.
9. The last half of the movie moved slowly.
10. The tornado blew down the enormous trees.
11. The kids cried and screamed, but their mother would not change her mind.
12. Give Mandy this mouse immediately!
13. Where did you get that bright orange shirt?
14. Rats! We are having cheese sandwiches for dinner again.
15. Did either you or Jorge read this letter?
16. Doris never knows which day of the week it is.
17. Rocky lives near the Hudson River.
18. Dean James punished the two unpleasant students.
19. Oh, I never get spinach or yams for breakfast anymore.
20. How did Maxie escape from that obnoxious bully?

18. SENTENCES

A. *Directions:* In the space at the end of each group of words, write **F** if it is a fragment, **R** if it is a run-on, and **S** if it is a sentence.
EXAMPLE: In the middle. __F__

1. Pip fell in love with Estella, however, she was cruel to him. ____

2. When the Mole became lost in the Wild Wood. ____
3. Bilbo Baggins did not particularly like adventures. ____
4. After Jane went to work for Mr. Rochester. ____
5. Scout and Jem looked up to Atticus, he was their father. ____
6. Exciting as the opening of *Treasure Island* is. ____
7. On Tuesday Christopher Robin ate lunch with Winnie-the-Pooh. ____

8. While Huck and Jim were drifting peacefully down the Mississippi River. ____
9. Annie gave Helen the gift of language, they were always friends after that. ____
10. Scrooge was very mean to Bob Cratchitt. ____
11. Do you remember how Beth March died in the book? ____
12. Laura and her family both in the woods and on the prairie. ____

13. The children were rather frightened of Aslan, nevertheless, they thought he was wonderful. ____
14. Miss Slighcarp treated Bonnie and Sylvia horribly. ____
15. Living on Prince Edward Island all those years, Anne Shirley. ____

16. Although the boy often missed Sounder. ____
17. Milo's adventures in the Lands Beyond changed his life. ____
18. Paddington was an unusual bear, I know that for sure. ____
19. Since Tom Thumb and Hunca Munca almost ruined the doll's house. ____
20. Mary discovered another garden, it was a secret one. ____

B. *Directions:* Depending on what type of sentence it is, write *simple* or *compound* in the space after each of the following sentences.
EXAMPLE: Coco loves green peppers, but I love anchovies.
____compound____

1. Abraham Lincoln was elected in 1860 and served as president during the Civil War. _____

2. Salvator couldn't see the stage, so he moved. _____

3. Alicia went to the adventure movie; it was exciting.
   _____

4. Tommy and Maria dug and hauled sand all day.
   _____

5. Where are you going, and why are you going there?
   _____

6. The family drove the sleigh over the river and through the woods.
   _____

7. Grandma came to my party on Friday. _____

8. Martina won the election for class president. _____

9. Yes, I am talking to you, Willie. _____

10. Bernice saw her down by the banks of the Ohio River.
    _____

11. The man looked like a ferocious pirate, but he was really very kind. _____

12. Pauline, Joanne, and I decided to fly to Europe and went the next day. _____

13. Buy a newspaper and bring it to me. _____

14. Robert Scott and his men died on the way back from the South Pole. _____

15. Look it up in the dictionary; you'll find it there.
    _____

16. Ken and Basil pooled their money and bought a giraffe.
    _____

17. Matu laughed at the joke, but he looked hurt too.
    _____

18. The wizard cast a spell on the handsome frog.
    _____

19. Are you going to the peace march, or will you miss it?
    _____

20. A cobra is a type of snake; it is extremely dangerous.
    _____

C. *Directions:* Each of the problems below contains two sentences. Using a semicolon, a colon, an appositive, or a conjunction, combine these two sentences into one sentence.

EXAMPLE: I love pickles.
I love olives.
I love pickles and olives.

1. Mr. Goldberg teaches history.
Mr. Goldberg is my favorite teacher.

_____

2. The test is on Thursday.
I studied hard for the test.

_____

3. Dan is clumsy.
Dan is also smart.

_____

4. I like several kinds of fruit.
I like pears, apples, plums, and grapes.

_____

5. Tony is my friend.
Tony got lost in the woods.

_____

6. Frieda enjoys the movies.
Frieda can't afford to go to the movies.

_____

7. Captain Ahab hated Moby Dick.
Moby Dick was a whale.

_____

8. Jake is going to Australia this summer.
He is also going to New Zealand.

_____

9. Anton entered the marathon.
Anton didn't finish the marathon.

_____

10. Rosa likes several outdoor sports.
Rosa likes hiking, skiing, and swimming.

_____

11. Edinburgh is the capital of Scotland.
Edinburgh is a lovely city.

_____

12. The Martians invaded our town.
    Bobby-Joe escaped from the Martians.

    _____

13. Miguel writes home every week.
    Miguel calls home every month.

    _____

14. Saturday morning was beautiful.
    It rained Saturday afternoon.

    _____

15. Ms. Najinsky went on a world tour.
    Ms. Najinsky visited China, Vietnam, Japan, and Korea.

    _____

16. My father is a truck driver.
    My father has been driving trucks for twenty years.

    _____

17. Paul watches television on Sundays.
    Sometimes Paul plays tennis on Sundays.

    _____

18. Elisa went to Hollywood.
    Elisa became a movie star.

    _____

19. Bing likes to sing songs.
    Bob likes to crack jokes.

    _____

20. The reporter criticized the president.
    The reporter's name is Wendy Williams.

    _____

19. PUNCTUATION

A. *Directions:* Insert the correct punctuation where it is needed in the following sentences. You may add 's when necessary.
EXAMPLE: I like the following animals: snails, lizards, and snakes.

1. Where are we going Chu Ling asked
2. No Lucy couldnt climb a tree that tall
3. Ive never eaten frogs moreover I never will
4. The golem is a creature in medieval Jewish legends the teacher said
5. Never You cant make me eat those beets Jake cried
6. Does Arnie belong to the engineers union
7. I like James Thurbers story The Catbird Seat
8. These are the main bodies of water rivers lakes and oceans
9. Yes she arrived on May 24 1927
10. Bernice asked me if Id seen the boys soccer team
11. Ill go to medical school Trini said and then Ill become a doctor
12. Rex went to the fair Sadie went with him
13. Ms. Melvin asked Why is your hair blue Sid
14. Apart from his uncle Abner didnt like his relatives
15. Drat said Theresa Why cant I learn this song
16. Jose asked whether its snowing here
17. I havent read Stuart Little however I have read Charlottes Web
18. Andre lives at 236 Lake Road Fisheye Montana
19. The mens club lost its building in a fire
20. My brother likes three flavors of ice cream chocolate strawberry and vanilla

B. *Directions:* The following sentences are partially punctuated. Insert the missing punctuation marks wherever necessary.
EXAMPLE: Jack went up the hill; Jill went too.

1. Did the slow green tortoise beat the hare?
2. The captain of our softball team Martina Smith is wonderful.
3. I told Marie "You are doing beautifully.
4. Yes there is a national writers union.
5. Did you ask why she couldnt be here, Kevin
6. I've been to Europe three times Leroy replied.
7. Pablo was late he couldn't play.
8. I saw the following animals in Alaska bear moose, and eagles.

9. Beatrice asked Tracy, her sister if she wanted to play
10. Flagstaff Arizona is my home town.
11. Below the waterfall fell down into the ravine.
12. June hates fish moreover, she hates fishing.
13. "Does Chuck always get up at 700 a.m.? she asked.
14. Yeats an Irish poet died in 1939.
15. "Ouch said Bernie. That shot hurt."
16. These are my favorite vegetables carrots, peas, and beans.
17. In October 1929 the stock market crashed said Mr. Tyson.
18. Wont you give me a hand Julie?
19. James wondered what Athens Greece was like.
20. Wayne looked at the headline then he gave the paper to Beth.

C. *Directions:* Make up ten sentences of your own that contain the forms of punctuation indicated in each problem.
EXAMPLE: apostrophe   I can't type.

1. semicolon _____
2. comma _____
3. quotation marks _____
4. colon _____
5. exclamation point _____
6. semicolon _____
7. quotation marks _____
8. question mark _____
9. colon _____
10. apostrophe _____

20. PREPOSITIONAL PHRASES

A. *Directions:* Put parentheses around each of the prepositional phrases in the following sentences. Then, depending on the function of that prepositional phrase, write **adjective** or **adverb** in the space provided at the end.

EXAMPLE: I walked (into the house.) _____adverb_____

1. The parakeet on the teapot is mine. _____

2. Chino's parents traveled around the world. _____

3. During intermission we bought some popcorn. _____

4. I want the book with the red cover. _____

5. Hester and Becky applied to the same college. _____

6. After the speech the politician shook people's hands.

_____

7. Wanda generally arrives at midnight. _____

8. In spite of my warnings, Tom stole the turkey. _____

9. The story about the deadly lottery disturbed me.

_____

10. Have you ever seen the man in the moon? _____

11. Like her sister, Dorothy hated pizza. _____

12. The climax of the play was suspenseful. _____

13. Don't ever put your socks under the bed again!

_____

14. The man behind the counter is my father. _____

15. Out of the tent emerged a rhinoceros. _____

16. Between television shows Lois made some tea.

_____

17. Have you ever read the book about the killer chipmunks?

_____

18. Mr. Claus drove the sled through the woods. _____

19. Since that night Tilly has looked sad. _____

20. Carol keeps a genie inside the lamp. _____

B. *Directions:* Put parentheses around the prepositional phrases in the following sentences. Then label them **ADJ** or **ADV** depending on their function.

ADV   ADJ

EXAMPLE: (After school) I bought a piece (of candy).

1. During World War II many people were uprooted from their homes.
2. The frogs in Walden Pond croaked throughout the night.
3. Millions of years ago dinosaurs walked on the earth.
4. On Mondays Rita bikes around the reservoir.
5. According to my older sister I belong inside a zoo.
6. The fish in the bathtub belongs to Arthur.
7. After the earthquake the mayor walked among the ruined buildings.
8. The woman beside the car voted against Governor Viper.
9. Will you take the book about witches up to the attic?
10. Apart from one slip at the beginning, Natasha danced brilliantly.
11. The baby in the basket slept until dinner.
12. Amid the growing noise Samantha slipped behind the curtains.
13. Because of your threats I will report you to the police.
14. Despite Maureen's cheering, the horse with spots lost the race.
15. The man on the roof crawled toward the chimney.
16. Frieda moved into the house by the bakery.
17. The family across the street moved in around May 1.
18. Instead of soda would you like some water with ice?
19. Throughout the recital Lulu scowled at her piano teacher.
20. The people above our apartment danced through the night.

C. *Directions:* Complete the sentences below by inserting prepositional phrases in the spaces. Then label them **ADJ** or **ADV** depending on their function.

ADV   ADV

EXAMPLE: <u>On Tuesday</u> Stu saw Jean <u>at the game</u>.

1. _____ Sherman flew his kite

_____ .

2. The dog _____ bit my friend

   _____ .

3. Melinda delivered the pizza _____

   and then returned _____ .

4. _____ I saw the girl _____

   _____ .

5. The car _____ skidded

   _____ .

6. Pascal likes to run _____ and

   _____ .

7. _____ Judy helped the old man

   _____ .

8. My favorite character _____

   reminds me of a photograph _____ .

9. Jan insisted _____ that we listen to

   the record _____ .

10. _____ Irma sang to the children

    _____ .

21. ERRORS

A. *Directions:* Each of the following sentences contains at least one error. Rewrite each sentence correctly in the space provided.

EXAMPLE: elmore is my pet mooses' name?

Elmore is my pet moose's name.

1. I love Grammar tests," Trixie said.

   _____

2. Janice called her three best friends; Dana, Rolla, and Sam.

   _____

3. The girls band could'nt get home in the blizzard.

   _____

4. I don't know it's name: furthermore, I don't care.

   _____

5. Billy, my brother went to the doctor's office.

   _____

6. Rick and Betsy goes on Tuesdays; but Bill never sees them.

   _____

7. Harry asked me "why Im standing on my head?"

   _____

8. My sister writes novels, so does I.

   _____

9. "One of those dogs have rabies," he screamed!

   _____

10. Do you know Trees; its a terrible poem.

    _____

11. Julius Caesar said "I came; I saw; and I conquered".

    _____

12. Why did randy say, I'll meet you at the river?"

    _____

13. The geeses' necks are black, with white rings.

    _____

14. My only duck Mabel, eat jelly beans' for dinner.

_____

15. "Meet me at my Gettysburg address" Abe said.

_____

16. There are a herd of cattle, in my back yard.

_____

17. We went to see Star wars; its a great movie

_____

18. Either the boys or I are going to Jame's birthday party.

_____

19. "Did you like the acrobats uniforms," Sandy wondered.

_____

20. One of the girls' play here every day, Im sure of it?

_____